I Know that My Redeemer Lives

I Know that My Redeemer Lives

Suffering and Redemption in the Book of Job

Ronald P. Hesselgrave

WIPF & STOCK · Eugene, Oregon

I KNOW THAT MY REDEEMER LIVES
Suffering and Redemption in the Book of Job

Copyright © 2016 Ronald P. Hesselgrave. All rights reserved. Except for brief quotations in critical publications or reviews, no part of this book may be reproduced in any manner without prior written permission from the publisher. Write: Permissions, Wipf and Stock Publishers, 199 W. 8th Ave., Suite 3, Eugene, OR 97401.

Wipf & Stock
An Imprint of Wipf and Stock Publishers
199 W. 8th Ave., Suite 3
Eugene, OR 97401

www.wipfandstock.com

PAPERBACK ISBN: 978-1-4982-8158-4
HARDCOVER ISBN: 978-1-4982-8160-7
EBOOK ISBN: 978-1-4982-8159-1

Manufactured in the U.S.A.   OCTOBER 5, 2016

Unless otherwise noted, Scripture is taken from the Holy Bible, New International Version. NIV®. Copyright © 1973, 1978, 1984 International Bible Society. Used by permission of Zondervan Bible Publishers.

Scripture translations labeled ESV® are from the Holy Bible, English Standard Version. Copyright © 2001 by Crossway Bible, a publishing ministry of Good News Publishers. Used by permission. All rights reserved.

Contents

List of Illustrations | vi
Preface | vii

Introduction | 1

Part One: Job and God's Redemptive Purpose | 17

CHAPTER 1   The Mission of God in the Book of Job | 19

Part Two: Job and Wisdom Literature | 31

CHAPTER 2   God's Ongoing Activity in His Creation | 33
CHAPTER 3   The Ambiguity and Unpredictability of Life | 40
CHAPTER 4   The Fear of God in Response to His Sovereignty | 49
CHAPTER 5   The Redemptive Grace of God | 56

Part Three: The Speeches in Job | 69

CHAPTER 6   Job's Friends | 71
CHAPTER 7   Job's Lament | 80
CHAPTER 8   Where is Wisdom to be Found? | 88
CHAPTER 9   Elihu's Theology | 98
CHAPTER 10   The Lord Speaks | 104

Conclusion: Towards a Practical Theology of Suffering | 114
Appendix: Discussion Guide | 123
Bibliography | 137

List of Illustrations

Figure 1 Basic Structure of Job | 4
Figure 2 Hermeneutical Spiral | 7
Figure 3 God's Mission, Job's Story, and the Reader's Story | 25

Preface

JOB IS ONE OF the most popular books in the Bible, as is indicated by the large number of commentaries and other studies on this ancient story. The reason for this popularity not only has to do with the fact that it addresses the universal human experience of suffering. Despite difficulties of interpretation, it is also a gripping story of one man's struggle to find meaning in the midst of personal tragedy. So, the reader might ask, "Why another book on Job?"

The approach to Job that I have adopted in this study differs from that of other studies in a number of respects. To begin with, the idea for this book has partially grown out of dialogues with missionary colleagues, many of whom are faced with the reality of suffering in their mission work. This is particularly true of missionaries who minister in an urban context and/or are engaged in holistic mission, which integrates evangelism and church planting with ministries of compassion and justice. Suffering is also the daily experience of missionaries who have been called to work in contexts of social and religious hostility. In his recent book, *Understanding Christian Mission: Participation in Suffering and Glory*, Scott Sunquist argues that, "Suffering is inescapable as a central element in God's redemption."[1] He writes that he has come to this conclusion, not only because it is a central theme in Scripture but also because of his personal encounters with the reality of suffering:

> [Having] started out our life fairly well protected from suffering, I was exposed to human suffering during our sojourn in Asia. The masses of people sleeping alongside the road in the metropolis of Madras (Chennai), the pictures of thousands suffering from disease and unhealthy water during the annual monsoon floods in

---

1. Sunquist, *Understanding Christian Mission*, xiii.

Preface

Bangladesh, and the millions of people living in squalor—drinking from the same river they bathe in—in Jakarta began to open my eyes to the reality of suffering. Then there came news reports from Christian leaders in Indonesia, Vietnam, Laos, India, and other countries of persecution from Muslim mobs, Communist governments, or Hindu fundamentalists . . . . The overwhelming and sustaining image that I came away with is of the suffering of Christians as Christianity has developed in each new region. Suffering is very much a part of Christian existence, as well as human existence in general.[2]

It is not commonly recognized that the book of Job has a missionary purpose in the sense that it is concerned with the "missio Dei," or God's mission in the world. In other words, the story of Job is about suffering and the "grand narrative" of God's redemptive purpose in history. This is the argument that I give in chapter one of this study. From this perspective, Job has particular relevance for the evangelistic efforts of missionaries around the world, especially in cases where they minister to persons who face innocent suffering of various kinds or are themselves targets of persecution.

Given this larger "missionary" purpose of Job, I suggest that this story is not just about Job's very personal and intense wrestling with suffering in the context of his relationship with God. Certainly, it is that. But Job's experience as an individual is in a very real sense also representative of the pain and vexation of humanity as a whole. Here, I agree with Robert Fyall's interpretation that central to the story of Job is a theology of creation which views all of creation as the scene of the battle between God and the forces of evil and looks forward to its final redemption.[3] There are others who adopt this particular reading of the story of Job.[4] But it is generally not emphasized. Yet such an interpretation opens up many new avenues of exploration and application for today. In this study I explore these themes of creation, evil, and God's sovereignty and redemption in Job against the backdrop of wisdom literature as a whole. I also attempt to show how the author's arrangement of the separate speeches highlight God's redemption, grace, justice, and purpose for creation; and how Job comes to see this in the crucible of suffering.

---

2. Ibid., xiv.

3. Fyall, *Now My Eyes Have Seen You*, 188–89.

4. See, for example, Reitman, *Unlocking Wisdom*, 170; and Vanhoozer, *Remythologizing Theology*, 47–49.

Preface

Another feature of Job which in my opinion is not sufficiently addressed is the social dimension of suffering. For instance, in seeking to understand and apply this compelling story it is important to observe that Job goes from being a very wealthy, influential, and respected member of the community to a poor man who is rejected by his peers and an object of contempt and ridicule. Like leprosy in Jesus' day, the painful sores that cover his body render him unclean and socially untouchable. The retribution principle that a man "reaps what he sows" only reinforces the belief that his suffering and attendant social ostracism is justified. From this perspective, the "dung heap" is symbolic of the social rejection of the very poor (such as the homeless), those with disabilities, and victims of AIDS, even by people within the church.[5] Of course, there are limits to such an interpretation. I make it clear in this book that we must avoid a strictly "liberation theology" perspective which views God's "preferential option for the poor" as the central message of Job. However, we must not go to the opposite extreme of avoiding altogether the theme of social justice in this book. Nor must we lose sight of the lesson (also emphasized in Job) that God is most often revealed in our pain, vulnerability, and weakness.

A final concern of this study is with the pastoral or practical value of the book of Job, both for caregivers (including counselors, pastors, and lay leaders) and those who may themselves be going through the valley of deep trauma and suffering. Many interpretations of Job focus on suffering as a problem of theodicy, or the justification of God's ways in cases of extreme human suffering. Such a reading of Job does not necessarily conflict with a more pastoral approach. In fact, I suggest that the two approaches can be complementary if sufficient attention is given to the particular needs of the sufferer at a given time. Nonetheless, I would argue that reading the book of Job from a strictly intellectual or theological standpoint runs the risk of misinterpreting and misapplying many segments of this ancient story, particularly Job's laments. In this study I have attempted to bring together theological and social-psychological insights in a way that deepens our understanding of suffering and provides the basis for a more comprehensive response to the needs of those who suffer. The reader will have to judge the extent to which I have been successful.

It should be apparent from what I have said that this study is intended for those in ministry (missionaries, pastors, counselors, and lay leaders), particularly those engaged in ministering to persons who experience

---

5. On this see Hubble, *Conversation on the Dung Heap*, 7–10.

Preface

various types of suffering and trauma in their lives. It is also intended for those who may themselves be in some way directly impacted by the fire of innocent suffering. But while individuals can benefit from personal study of Job using this book, this is not its sole purpose. It is increasingly acknowledged by those who are concerned with "pastoral theology" that ministry to those who suffer is not just the task of professional caregivers or church leaders, it is the responsibility of the entire church body. Mutual support and encouragement are crucial to the collective well-being of the church as a whole (Gal 6:2). Given this need to equip and empower lay care-givers, it is hoped this book will be used for group Bible study within the local church.

My wife, Kathi, and I are part of a multicultural church in which sufferings of various types are the daily lot for many members of the congregation. Collectively, as brothers and sisters in the body of Christ, we are learning what it means to be informed by what Michael Gorman refers to as "a spirituality of the cross."[6] This was, as Gorman argues, the focus of Paul's gospel and life. Paul's life mission was to "order the lives of Christian congregations by pulling everything into the tremendous gravitational field of the cross."[7] This approach to spirituality does not merely ask what the text says, but also what it enjoins us to believe (faith), to do (love), and to anticipate (hope).[8] These three spiritual disciplines of the Christian life are foundational to a biblical approach to suffering. This is beautifully expressed in the following poem penned by one of the members of our congregation, entitled "Blue Lament."[9]

> Blue Lament are you really heaven sent?
> Joy and gladness have suddenly turned into sadness.
> *How can this be?*
> *Why can't He see?*
> God Creator of the universe
> Inspirer of Verses and Holy Truth
> The REAL proof of those who came before us . . .
> Of what's to gain and what's to come . . .
> Blue Lament

---

6. Gorman, *Cruciformity*, 5.
7. Elliot, *Liberating Paul*, 93. Quoted in Gorman, *Cruciformity*, 5.
8. Ibid.
9. I am grateful to Jennifer Handyside for giving me permission to use this poem.

Preface

Comes in the form of hearing out others
Their pains and sorrows
Not to mention our *own* that sneak up
And Consume us.
Romans 12:15 tells us to "Rejoice with those who rejoice"
And to "mourn with those who mourn."
With those who are Scorned or Possibly SOCIALLY REJECTED.
OR who have faced the unexpected.
Blue Lament
It's okay to be *seen*
Amidst a MEAN and Cold, cruel world,
That's moving so SO fast.
That makes the WONDERERS Ask
Why . . . has . . . God . . . Cast . . . THIS Gloom Upon US?
Like in the stripping away of Job.
Like in the weeping of Jeremiah.
Like in the cries of David.
Like in the griefs of Naomi.
Like in the suffering of Jesus.
Blue Lament
Pour out . . . Pour out
Cry out . . . Cry out
And cleanse your soul . . . and KNOW that
The Lord is Good to those whose Hope is in him . . .
For it is good to sit Alone in Silence
And no one is Cast out forever.
Though he brings grief he will show
COMPASSION . . . so Great is his UNFAILING LOVE
Blue Lament there is HOPE.

    This book would not have been possible without the support and encouragement of family, friends, and co-workers. I am grateful to those in my biological family as well as to fellow brothers and sisters in the larger spiritual family who, even in times of personal difficulty and suffering, are an example of what it means to live in "a manner worthy of the gospel of Christ." (Phil 1:27) This book is dedicated to you. Although I alone am responsible for the final content, I have benefited greatly from the insights

Preface

of others who have read all or portions of the manuscript. I am particularly indebted to pastor Luke McFadden, and to my missionary colleague, Jim Baker, who have offered much needed critical feedback. Many thanks also to both Lore Cooper and John McFadden for their painstaking and thorough work of editing the entire manuscript. Finally, I am profoundly grateful to Kathi Hesselgrave for tolerating my long hours at the computer and so generously supporting me with her words of encouragement and advice. I could not have found a better partner, in life or in ministry.

Introduction

I BEGIN WITH A brief explanation of why the story of Job resonates with me and why I have chosen to write this book. My wife, Kathi, and I have a number of family members, relatives, and close friends who have faced, or are facing, serious illness and other painful and life-altering circumstances. So the message of Job is not without direct relevance for us personally.[1] But there are other reasons why I am particularly drawn to this ancient story. In the ministry to address human trafficking which we helped to form, Kathi and I have heard heart-wrenching stories of horrific abuse. I also serve as a home-based missionary with a denominational mission[2] that, as part of its evangelistic and church planting efforts, ministers holistically to victims of trafficking, poverty, social discrimination, and other types of physical, emotional, and spiritual trauma. A number of years ago, I was also part of a crisis response ministry through the same denomination[3] that provided relief to victims in the wake of Hurricane Katrina. We encountered story after story of harrowing experiences by survivors. One man told of swimming for hours in water filled with debris, deadly toxins, garbage, and dead bodies after losing his own home and some members of his family to the storm. Chances are, you have also been impacted by suffering in some way. You may be reading this book at least in part because you have experienced some type of traumatic event in your life, or are in close relationship with someone who has. Or you may be ministering in some way to those who

---

1. I should add that while I am currently in relatively good health I myself have type II diabetes and have recently been diagnosed with the early stages of Parkinson's disease.

2. EFCA ReachGlobal, which is the international mission of the Evangelical Free Church of America.

3. EFCA Crisis Response responds to disasters, both nationally and internationally.

INTRODUCTION

are going through the valley of suffering—whether it be deep loss, abuse, or pronounced physical or mental illness.

The fact is, none of us is a stranger to suffering; which is why Job is one of the most discussed books in the Bible. Commonly recognized as a literary masterpiece, it has been described as a "defining myth" for the twentieth century that "has captivated the human imagination and has forced its readers to wrestle with the most painful realities of human existence."[4] For example, Elie Wiesel uses the story of Job to help people who survived or were close to survivors of the Holocaust. For him, the Holocaust survivor's story of unjust suffering is Job's story.[5] In *The Book of Job: When Bad Things Happen to a Good Person*, Harold Kushner similarly uses the biblical story as a moral example of how to respond to random tragedy. In the last chapter from his book he quotes from a speech he made to a New Orleans congregation on the first anniversary of Katrina: "You want to know why something like this could happen to you. I can give you the answer in six words, God is moral, nature is not."[6] Later in his speech, he asked, "Where was God when your city was struck? His was the still, small voice moving some residents to go out in their rowboats and rescue you from your rooftops."[7] Recently, a group of television and movie actors came together to perform an adapted version of the biblical tale to commemorate the one-year anniversary of devastation caused by Hurricane Sandy. The two-hour performance included a 30-minute reading followed by a community discussion where residents of Red Hook, New York and first responders discussed their experiences with Sandy in relation to the poem.[8]

These cases help to explain the universal appeal of the book of Job. They also illustrate the difficulties inherent in properly interpreting and applying the message of this portion of Scripture. While Job is one of the most talked-about books of the Bible, it is also one of the least understood. Greg Parsons notes that many preachers tend to shy away from preaching the book because of its complex dialogue and hard-to-understand passages. If they do preach from Job, it is mainly to present an oversimplified picture of Job as a model for modern-day believers to "be patient" in the midst of trials. This ignores the many hard questions raised by Job concerning

---

4. Schreiner, *Where Shall Wisdom be Found?*, 1.
5. Mathewson, "Between Testimony and Interpretation," 17.
6. Kushner, *Book of Job*, 197.
7. Ibid., 198.
8. Venugopal, "Actors Read Biblical Book of Job," 1.

the mystery of innocent suffering. "Yet the candid record that Job began to question God strikes a chord familiar to humankind. To ignore Job's question 'why?' (see 3:11, 12, 20; 10:18; 13:24; 24:1) and his search for God's answer is to ignore basic issues of life everyone must face."[9] At the same time, the questions that Job raises and the answers he seeks are framed completely within the context of belief in a sovereign God who is just in all of his ways. Therefore, from the perspective of this book, it is illegitimate to seek solutions outside of God's revelation of himself.[10] As John Walton reminds us, it is imperative that we ask the right questions. Perhaps we do not fully recognize the answers the book offers because we have asked the wrong questions—or, more accurately, the less important questions. Ultimately, the most important question is not why persons suffer, or even how we should respond to suffering:

> Our questions about suffering inevitably lead to God, for when we go through difficult times in life, there is no one else to question—he is the one whose ways we seek to understand. When we ask "Why me?" we are in effect asking "How does God work?" We may start out asking why we deserved this, but ultimately the question we arrived at is, "What kind of God are you?"[11]

Structure and Purpose of the Book of Job

The first and most fundamental step in properly understanding any book of the Bible and interpreting specific passages within it is to look at the book in its entirety. The old adage that one should not lose the forest for the trees is a reminder that we can easily become so engrossed in the particular details of a book that we lose sight of the bigger picture. The dangers inherent in this tendency are particularly applicable to the book of Job. Preachers or teachers who try to pull out some principle based on one particular verse in Job without an awareness of the immediate and overall context risk distorting the meaning of its story and misrepresenting its message for today.[12]

---

9. Parsons, "Guidelines," 393–94.
10. Andersen, *Job*, 67.
11. Walton, *Job*, 20.
12. Parsons, "Guidelines," 295. Parsons gives as an example sermons or lessons that have given an idealized portrayal of Job's faith based on the famous verse, 19:15 "I know that my Redeemer lives and that in the end he will stand upon the earth." This image of Job is really a distortion of the overall story presented in the book of Job.

Introduction

We can best understand the book of Job, then, if we take a bird's-eye view. This is done at two levels: 1) identifying the book's overall structure, noting the ebb and flow of its thought development; and 2) determining its biblical theology, or the major emphasis of the author.[13] The basic structure of the book of Job (fig. 1) consists of a series of poetic speeches (3:1–42:6) bracketed by a prologue (chs. 1–2) and an epilogue (42:7–17). The prologue narrates how Job lost his possessions, family, and health through a succession of events. This testing of Job features repeated alternations between scenes in heaven involving interviews of God with the Accuser[14] (1:6–12; 2:1–6) and scenes on earth in which the Accuser brings wanton destruction on Job (1:13–22; 2:7–10). The poetic body (3:1–42:6) consists of dialogues (disputations between Job and his three friends), laments, discourses, narratives, hymns (to name a few of the literary devices)—all of which are essential to developing the argument of the book.[15] The epilogue describes the final outcome in which the Lord renders a final verdict on Job and his friends (42:7–9) and restores Job's prosperity (42:10–16).

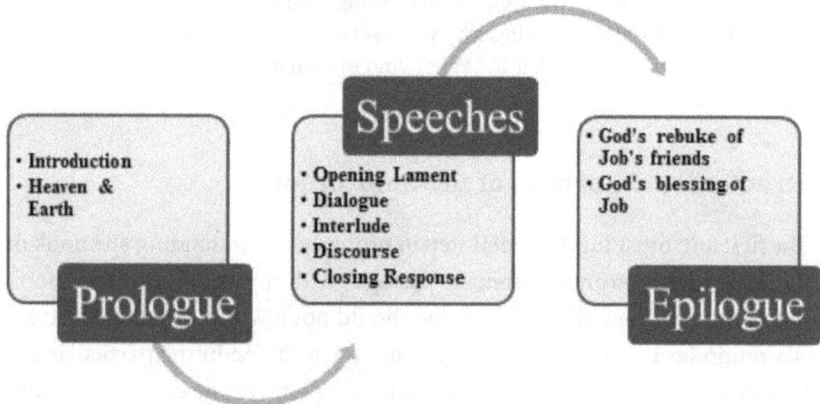

Figure 1 Basic Structure of Job

Citing the variety of literary genres, various commentators have maintained that the book of Job is not the work of one author but the product of a number of different authors, with some sections such as the poetic speeches being later additions to the original narrative (the frame), or vice

---

13. Osborne, *Hermeneutical Spiral*, 354.

14. I am going to refer to Satan throughout as "the Accuser." For a discussion of the identity of the Accuser, see chapter 3.

15. Walton, *Job*, 27.

versa.[16] However, closer examination of the inner structure of this book reveals a symmetry and balance similar to that of a classical musical composition which argues strongly for one author.[17] As Walton points out in his commentary on Job,[18] the three sets of speeches in the dialogue section (chaps. 4–27) are balanced by three sets of speeches in the discourse section (chaps. 29–41). Job's opening lament (chap. 3), which leads into the dialogue with his three friends, is balanced by his responses to God (esp. 42:1–6) which emerge from the discourse section. The wisdom hymn in chapter 28 is probably an interlude which is best attributable to Job. It serves as a transition that brings formal closure to the debate between Job and his three friends.[19]

Each of these sections is important for understanding the overall purpose of the book. The prologue sets the stage for the story of Job as a whole. The basic problem of the book is raised by the Accuser's question in 1:9—"Does Job fear God for nothing?" Spiritually, this question centers on the motivation for Job's piety. It suggests that God's rewards are the incentive for righteous conduct.[20] Job's suffering then becomes a test case of true faith. Morally, the policy under examination is the principle of retribution, that a person "reaps what he sows." The experience of Job—who is described at the outset as the most blameless and upright man on earth (1:8)—forces the reader to rethink simplistic beliefs that the righteous always prosper and the wicked always suffer. Theologically, and ultimately, the issue that is raised is how we are to understand God when we and those we love suffer. At the emotional level, this combination of questions is bound up with feelings of despair, hope, sorrow, frustration, anger, and sympathy which are displayed by Job and his presumed comforters as we move through the story. These emotions are particularly evident in Job's laments and in the exchanges between him and his friends, which become more heated yet shorter in each subsequent round. As James Reitman states, "The escalating invective exchanged by Job and his friends reflects faulty notions of God's justice and redemptive grace . . . The honest reader will allow Job's plight to challenge stereotyped views of God's justice and to expose the limits of

---

16. Walton, *Job*, 28.
17. Andersen, *Job*, 21.
18. Walton, *Job*, 28–29.
19. See Hooks, *Job*, 30. On his point I disagree with Walton's assessment that the wisdom poem in chapter 28 is an interjection by the narrator. See Walton, *Job*, 29.
20. Ibid., 21.

human wisdom and our ignorance regarding God's sovereign purposes in suffering."[21] The poem on wisdom (chapter 28) gives a brief respite from the turbulence before and after it.[22] Structurally, this chapter marks a very gradual swing toward a focus on Job's relationship and interaction with God which culminates in the climactic speeches of the Lord and Job's final response of faith (42:1–6). Thus, while there are many sub-themes and subplots in this book, its primary overarching purpose is to show God's grace, justice, providence, and purpose for creation and how these are to be understood in the crucible of suffering.[23]

Applying the Book of Job Today

There is a tendency in some Christian circles to emphasize a simple reading of the Bible that asks two basic questions: First, what does the passage say to me? Secondly, how can I apply it to my life? Those who promote this approach argue that, often, too much attention is given to professional scholarly interpretations of the Bible which distract people from the plain meaning of the text and its relavence to their lives. We should, it is argued, place less emphasis on commentaries, word studies, and the like. Instead, we need to get back to simply reading the Bible prayerfully and devotionally, making relevant applications to our lives and obeying what it tells us to do.[24]

There are both strengths and weaknesses to this approach. One problem with this perspective is that often there is not a simple correspondence between what we *think* a given text says and what it really means. Gordon Fee and Douglas Stuart raise the issue of "pre-understanding:"

> We . . . tend to think that *our understanding* is the same thing as the Holy Spirit's or human author's *intent*. However, we invariably bring *to* the text all that we are, with all of our experiences, culture, and prior understandings of words and ideas. Sometimes what we

---

21. Reitman, *Unlocking Wisdom*, 74 and 76.
22. Andersen, *Job*, 20.
23. See Fyall, *Now My Eyes Have Seen You*, 187–90.
24. An example of this approach is the *Life Application Study Bible* published by Zondervan. The study notes differ from a traditional study Bible in that they emphasize living out the principles of Scripture rather than simply looking at the historical details of the time period.

Introduction

bring to the text, unintentionally to be sure, leads us astray, or else causes us to read all kinds of foreign ideas into the text.[25]

In addition to this horizon of the reader there is also the horizon of the text itself—for although the Bible is God's inspired Word and has eternal relevance, it was written by human authors within a particular historical and cultural context. The text is therefore conditioned by the language, time, and culture in which it was transmitted. This context must be properly understood if we are to correctly grasp the original *intended meaning* of the author.[26]

At the same time, a proper interpretation of the text (or what is often referred to as *exegesis*) can never be an end in itself. Advocates of a simple reading and application of the text are right in pointing out that we can get so hung up on properly identifying the original intended meaning of the text that we never get around to applying it to our lives. Or, if we do apply it, we can do so in a manner that is shallow, ineffective, and does not lead to real life change. We must therefore engage in a twofold process of understanding what the text meant *then and there* and then hearing and applying it in the *here and now*.[27]

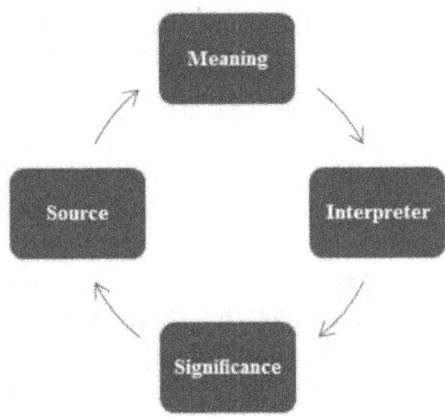

Figure 2 Hermeneutical Spiral

---

25. Fee and Stuart, *How to Read the Bible*, 7.
26. Ibid., 20–22.
27. Ibid., 21.

Introduction

Grant Osborne explains this twofold process of understanding the text and applying it in terms of a "hermeneutical spiral" (Fig. 2). The intended meaning of the text is important in its own right. But it is not complete until the significance of the biblical data has been determined. At the same time, the significance of the biblical text must be grounded in the original source or context of the passage.[28]

Since Job contains both narrative and poetic dialogue, there are also some features of what Osborne calls "narrative criticism" which are applicable in properly interpreting and applying this book. A point that has already been made is that it is important to read through the entire biblical narrative to catch the "drama and power" of the story as different elements fit together to form a "holistic panorama."[29] A narrative also contains a narrator who functions as the "invisible speaker" in the text and is invariably indistinguishable from God who inspires him. In Job the narrator has at least two important functions of which the reader needs to be aware:[30] First, he presents and interacts with the different "points of view" which are represented by various characters in the narrative. As Osborne observes, "a story usually has multiple perspectives as the narrator like a movie camera zeros in on one aspect then another in developing the plot, thereby guiding the reader in several meaning directions at the same time."[31] In the book of Job the various characters (Job, Eliphaz, Bildad, Zophar, Elihu) as well as the Lord's speeches all present a point of view on Job's suffering. In conjunction with the above observation, the narrator may also provide "inside information" on the thoughts and feelings of the characters, relate the story from various vantage points, and enable the reader to "listen in" on dialogues that one would never hear in the normal world. For example (as we will see) the fact that the reader (but not Job) is privy to the dialogue between God and the Accuser which takes place at the beginning of the story is important in teaching valuable theological lessons.

At the same time, it is important to be aware of the fact that narratives do not teach doctrine directly. While this does not mean that we cannot learn doctrine or derive "supra-cultural" principles from biblical narratives, such teachings are usually implicit. Biblical narratives often illustrate what is taught more clearly in other portions of Scripture. A related point

---

28. Osborne, *Hermeneutical Spiral*, 324.
29. Ibid., 154.
30. Ibid., 156–57.
31. Ibid., 156.

is that by nature narratives do not answer all of our theological questions. Thus, while the book of Job gives valuable insights of how to respond to suffering in the world and how we ought to understand God in relation to suffering, it is not a full theological treatise on *why* people suffer.[32]

Three Perspectives on Job

At this point it will be helpful to briefly discuss several different perspectives on the book of Job. Each of these perspectives reflects a different pre-understanding which stems from one's experience and from differing theological systems or models. The three perspectives I will look at briefly are that: 1) Job proclaims the incomprehensibility and sovereignty of God; 2) suffering is the "back door" to God's blessings; and 3) God is the defender of the poor and oppressed. I have chosen these perspectives, not because they are the only possible interpretations of Job, but because of their influence within Christian circles today.

The Incomprehensibility and Sovereignty of God

This perspective, which is heavily influenced by John Calvin's interpretation of the book of Job, is concerned with showing that Job's purpose in suffering is twofold. First, through Job's experience of suffering God's glory and sovereignty is demonstrated and his justice defended before those who would presumptively question or judge his hidden motives. And, secondly, suffering has "medicinal" value. That is, it refines Job's righteousness by deepening the spiritual qualities of reverence for God and submission to his providence, patience, repentance, joy, self-denial, trust, humility, and preparation for heaven.[33] This view emphasizes that everything that happens—even unjustified and innocent suffering—finds a place in the eternal counsel of God which is grounded in his goodness. God's providence therefore has a therapeutic character in that it communicates hope and comfort to people. There are times when the righteous suffer for no apparent reason and when they cannot understand God's intentions. In such times, one must acknowledge that God's ways are incomprehensible and trust in

---

32. Walton, *Job*, 23.

33. See Thomas, *Proclaiming the Incomprehensible God*, 225–40; and Potgieter, "Perspectives on the Doctrine of Providence in Some of Calvin's Sermons on Job," 36–38. John Piper also adopts this interpretation of Job.

his "hidden justice." From this perspective, Job's exaggerated laments and complaints before God are mostly manifestations of self-righteousness and pride. Job's confession at the end of the book confirms that: 1) God is absolutely sovereign; 2) God's wisdom is above our own; and 3) Job was guilty of the sin of pride in questioning God. God's final restoration of Job's health, family, and possessions in response to Job's confession shows that repentance and faith receive the forgiveness and grace of God.

Suffering as a "Back Door" to God's Blessing

The "prosperity gospel" promises success, blessing, and prosperity for those who trust and obey God. The main condition for receiving the abundance of material blessing is a faith in God that he will keep his promises and act. Advocates of this perspective argue that the experience of Job actually confirms this truth. For, although he is stricken with poverty, the death of family members, and sickness, at the end God rewards his faith by giving him twice as much as he had before (42:10).[34] Of the three perspectives, this one has the least validity, although variations of it are accepted by many. The weakness of this interpretation is evident in the fact that the whole point of Job is to question the dogma of divine retribution—that the righteous always prosper and the wicked are always punished—which is held by Job's three friends. The corrective provided by Calvin's emphasis on God's sovereignty is that man's relationship to God is not a "business contract" between two equals in which God is obligated to reward faith on our terms. God's restoration of Job's prosperity at the end of the book is not a reward or payment but a free gift based solely on his sovereign grace.

However, a more moderate and nuanced version of this perspective argues that the main theme of Job is "that God will ultimately bless the righteous man with prosperity when he trusts the Lord to the end and when he understands that the blessing is not his own but God's."[35] This version of the prosperity gospel downplays the emphasis of many prosperity theologians on "health and wealth" and defines success as "achieving

---

34. Kenneth Hagin states, "If you think you are another Job that means you'll be one of the richest men around. You'll have twice as much as you've ever had, and you will be healed and live to be old. Job lived one hundred .years after the events recorded in the Bible. If you are another Job, you are going to prosper." See Hagin, "Faith for Prosperity," 1.

35. Lee, "Case for Prosperity Theology," 26–39.

Introduction

God's goal for us"—a goal which is ultimately rooted in that which pleases God. Supporters of this more moderate view do not deny that suffering can be a means through which God brings discipline and correction, but they emphasize the positive and active role of faith in overcoming suffering. The promise of Job as well as other portions of the Old and New Testaments is that a person who suffers can overcome the sufferings through positive faith in God's love and mercy and live with hope for the future.

God as Defender of the Poor and Oppressed

Unlike the previous two perspectives, which focus on Job's personal experience of faith, this perspective focuses on Job as an "archetypal" figure who represents the unjust suffering of the innocent in the world.[36] It represents what might be termed a "theodicy at the margins."[37] The term "margins" refers to the marginalized of society—those who are underprivileged and powerless. A theodicy at the margins therefore looks at the problem of evil and suffering through the lens of "real life" experiences of exploitation and oppression—such as domestic violence, economic exploitation, and racism. It sees God as a defender of the poor widow, the alien, and orphan. Job is therefore seen as providing an ancient analogue to contemporary situations of injustice and exploitation.

Whereas Calvin (and those influenced by his theology) tend to view Job's laments as expressions of rebellion and pride, this perspective views them more positively as the lens through which we can recover that part of the biblical tradition which compassionately embraces and responds to the pain of those who suffer. Job gradually comes to see that he is not alone in his suffering, but shares it with all of the poor and oppressed. In identifying with all who suffer unjustly he becomes a "rebellious believer" whose "rebellion is against the suffering of the innocent, against a theology that justifies it, and even against the depiction of God that such a theology conveys."[38] Job's friends, on the other hand, express an individualistic theology that is out of touch with reality and justifies the position of the rich. The key to understanding this ancient story comes at the end when God justifies Job and condemns his friends. Job, for his part, repents in dust and ashes as he gains new insight into God's just governance of the world.

36. Gutierrez, *On Job*, xviii.
37. See Scott, "Theodicy at the Margins," 149–52.
38. Gutierrez, *On Job*, 14.

INTRODUCTION

The Perspective and Scope of this Study

It is clear from the above discussion that a person's pre-understanding influences both the interpretation and methods that one uses to interpret the book of Job. This does not necessarily mean that we are left with a relativistic pluralism of viewpoints. Different competing perspectives can be mutually correcting. Opposing models can force us to identify our own blind spots and re-examine the basis and structure of our theological assumptions. Ultimately, this drives us back to the text to see anew what Scripture actually teaches.[39] In what follows I will make some brief observations related to each of the above perspectives. I will then describe the approach and perspective that I take in this study.

Obviously, there is a strong emphasis in Job on the providence, sovereignty, and transcendence of God. However, a one-sided concern with this aspect of the book of Job can lead to interpretations which focus almost exclusively on reconciling the reality of evil with divine goodness and ominipotence. Studies of Calvin's sermons on Job, for example, have found that at times he descends into tortuous abstract theologizing in defending divine sovereignty that lacks a pastoral sensitivity to the reality and depth of human suffering. This is perhaps most apparent in Calvin's harsh criticisms of Job's exaggerated laments and complaints before God. On a more positive note, however, his stress on divine providence in Job points to an eschatological hope in times when history appears chaotic and God's rule cannot be discerned. God's redemptive purpose in response to evil in his creation (which is highlighted in the divine speeches) lies at the heart of Job's theology.[40]

In one respect, the more blatant form of the prosperity gospel which is found especially in the United States has little to offer in properly interpreting and applying the story of Job. We can agree with Walter Kaiser that, "The preoccupation of the gospel of affluence with material wealth is more of a sign of its sociological roots than of its biblical exegesis."[41] As has already been noted, Job's experience as an innocent sufferer is a refutation of overly simplistic applications of the retribution principle. At another level, however, the prosperity interpretation of Job does raise the question of how

---

39. Osborne, *Hermeneutical Spiral*, 307.

40. Fyall clearly brings out this dimension in Job's theology. He rightly argues that the divine speeches in chapters 38–41 must control the interpretation of this book (*Now My Eyes Have Seen You*, 18).

41. Kaiser, "Old Testament Promise," 162.

Introduction

the principle of retribution functions in Job relative to other wisdom literature such as Proverbs, which seems to teach that righteous living and faith invariably lead to divine blessing. I will take up this question in chapters two and five of this study. The more moderate forms of prosperity theology also have value in pointing to the positive role that faith plays in suffering. This further raises the more practical/pastoral question, "How is faith in God sustained in the midst of radical suffering?" Both the Calvinist and moderate forms of prosperity teaching help us see the redemptive function of suffering in the book of Job. I will argue that this is the contribution of Elihu's speeches which prepare the reader for the theophany in chapters 38–41. One important caveat, however, is that the redemptive value of suffering does not in any way negate or justify the evil of violence toward others; nor does it mean that people should endure violence that they can escape.[42]

In my opinion, a weakness in many treatments of the book of Job is a failure to see the social justice vision in this story. Walter Brueggemann observes that the role of "social evil" in Job and other biblical texts is often "bracketed out" when we come to the question of theodicy. David Pleins further argues, "We need to explore the social vision of Job that emerges from the dialogue, for this social vision is truly the heart of the text."[43] This is the value of the "theodicy at the margins" perspective. In my estimation, this vision of social justice in response to evil is particularly important in understanding Job's laments. It is also an important corrective to some emphases on the spiritual and "medicinal" value of suffering which "sacramentalize" suffering and powerlessness and encourage submission to unjust suffering rather than liberation from socio-political oppression.[44]

---

42. On this see Gorman, *Cruciformity*, 378–79. In saying that suffering can be "redemptive" I am suggesting that suffering can lead to a deeper understanding and experience of God's providence, love, and grace. God meets us in our pain, weakness, and powerlessness. I am not at all endorsing the Catholic view that suffering is salvific or has value in remitting sins.

43. Pleins, *Social Visions of the Hebrew Bible*, 500.

44. In giving a theological response to the global violence against women and girls, Elizabeth Gerhardt rightly argues that instruction regarding the reality of suffering in Christian's lives has been used "as an ideological tool to maintain power over women's and girls' lives. Too many times abused women have reported that teaching and counsel on the subject of suffering have led them to remain in abusive homes. They have been told that their suffering should be 'offered up to God' and that suffering will 'build up' their character. This is a horrific perversion of the teaching of the cross. The pain inflicted on women and girls is not salvific and does not make one holy. This type if suffering is a

Introduction

At the same time, a "theodicy at the margins" perspective runs the risk of elevating some forms of oppression and suffering in ways that cause one to lose sight of or ignore other types of suffering—such as that caused by a major life-threatening illness, disability, or old age. While it may be true that suffering often disproportionately affects the poor and marginalized, no one social group has a corner on affliction. It is also important to keep in mind that the story of Job focuses on God's relationship to Job as a *righteous* man—one whose life is oriented around faith in God and his ways. This does not mean that God is indifferent to the suffering of the unbelieving poor, broken, and downtrodden wherever they exist—or that this should not be an area of practical concern for Christians. Throughout the book of Job and Scripture as a whole it is assumed that God loves and cares for his entire creation. Nonetheless, the particular focus of this book is on the response to suffering of the righteous—those whose faith is in God and who are called by his name.[45] In the next chapter I will argue that an important part of the interpretative framework for Job is God's mission and his covenant with Israel.

Given the above observations, the particular focus of this study will be on the practical or pastoral implications of the theology of suffering which is found in the book of Job. It is assumed throughout this study that there is a unitary theology comprised of various motifs of divine sovereignty, providence, creation, evil, faith, and redemption that underlie this story.

---

result of the oppressor's sin and cultural and religious supports for the degradation and abuse of women and girls." Gerhardt, *The Cross and Gendercide*, 100.

45. At this point, it might be helpful to briefly discuss Gutierrez's perspective of liberation theology as it relates to his interpretation of Job. In *On Job* Gutierrez argues that God has a "preferential option for the poor" (94). We can agree that a central concern of Scripture is that God is a God of justice who sides with the oppressed against those who perpetrate injustice. However, Gutierrez (and other proponents of a theology of liberation) employ this concept in support of "soteriological praxis," or cooperation with God in "the ongoing transformation of history" to bring liberation from oppression (*On Job*, 94–103). This view of God's preferential option for the poor has a number of theological ramifications. First, it obliterates the distinction found throughout the Old Testament (as well as the New) between those who are God's people and those who are not. Secondly, it ultimately reduces salvation to the socio-political liberation of the poor. Third, it replaces the priority of the text (i.e., Scripture) as the final arbiter of truth with the priority of the context, namely the experience of oppression by the poor. And finally, instead of seeing the church as the central place of kingdom expression it views the world as the primary locus of kingdom activity as there is the transformation of humanity into a new humanity and the world into a just society. In each of these respects I believe Gutierrez's argument is theologically deficient.

Introduction

These theological motifs are of crucial significance for understanding the book of Job. However, these motifs do not operate in abstraction from real-life situations of suffering. The problem of innocent suffering is not simply an intellectual exercise. It also has experiential and pastoral dimensions. Therefore, in interpreting and applying the book of Job to our lives we must look at the intersection between philosophical, systematic, practical, and pastoral theology.[46]

Finally, a word should be said regarding the organization of this study. To encourage reflection on the practical implications of Job, at the end of each chapter I focus on real life applications of some of the ethical and theological principles that are found in this ancient story. The appendix to this book also contains questions on each chapter with guidelines for discussion so that it can be used as a ten-to twelve-week group Bible study. This book is not intended as a full-length verse-by-verse commentary. Rather, specific themes have been chosen for discussion. In part one I locate the book of Job within the larger context of God's mission in the world. In part two I identify some themes that the book of Job shares with wisdom literature generally. In part three I focus on different theologies of suffering that are represented by the main characters in this ancient drama. This study concludes with some observations on developing a practical theology of suffering based on the book of Job.

---

46. See Scott, "Theodicy at the Margins," 152.

PART ONE

Job and God's Redemptive Purpose

PREDICTIONS ABOUT THE END of the civilized world are increasingly common in both scientific literature and popular culture. Hollywood films such as *Deep Impact* (1998) and *The Road* (2006) depict cataclysmic events that bring an end to the world as we know it and force the remaining humans to resort to living in caves, scavenging, and cannibalism to survive. In *Armageddon* (1998) the plot centers on a rogue asteroid the size of Texas that will collide with the earth in 18 days. In a last ditch effort to avert an "extinction level event," NASA dispatches astronauts to detonate a nuclear weapon on the surface of the asteroid. In the movie *The Maze* (1999) the world is taken over by machines with artificial intelligence.

Various well-known scientists have also expressed pessimism about the fate of the civilized world. In *The Universe in a Nutshell* Stephen Hawking speculates that "by 2600 the world's population will be standing shoulder to shoulder, and the electricity use will make the Earth glow red hot."[47] Sir Martin Rees similarly speculates on future risks to human civilization, and concludes that the odds "are no better than fifty-fifty that our present civilization on Earth will survive to the end of the century."[48]

Does the book of Job have anything to say to these doomsday scenarios? I will argue that it does. Most studies of this book concentrate on Job's personal experience of suffering in the context of his relationship to God. While this is indeed an important facet of Job's overall message, the case can be made for a more holistic reading of Job as a depiction of disorder,

---

47. Quoted in Wilkinson, *Christian Eschatology*, 1.
48. Ibid.

pain, and evil within creation and God's ultimate response of grace and redemption. As Robert Fyall writes:

> In microcosm, the flow of the book reflects that of the canon itself. The 'blessedness' of the first few verses and the greater blessedness of the last few verses frame a profound struggle with the mysteries of creation, during which Job longs for the created order to be dissolved (ch. 3), expresses both awe and dismay at its mysteries (ch.. 9), uses profound language of worship (ch. 26) and wrestles with the great theological issues of wisdom and creation (ch. 28).[49]

This interpretation places the book of Job firmly within the context of the Bible's overall plotline.[50] The story of Job is connected with the larger Biblical narrative which depicts the cosmic struggle between God and Satan, and looks forward to Satan's eventual defeat and the creation of the "new heaven and new earth."[51] At its heart, then, the book of Job has a "missional" focus. It is part of the *missio Dei* ("mission of God"), or the progressive revelation of God's purpose and mission in history.[52]

---

49. Fyall, *Now My Eyes Have Seen You*, 188.
50. Ibid.
51. Ibid., 23–25, 182, 189.
52. See Waters, "Missio Dei," 19–35.

1

The Mission of God in the Book of Job

A SIMPLE READING OF the book of Job is that it is the story of a man of good works and faith who is struck down by a series of terrible adversities. The purpose of the book is to demonstrate the sovereignty of God over all areas of life and the importance of humble submission to his will even in the most difficult circumstances. While there is much to be said for this interpretation, as I have already noted, a deeper reading suggests that there is more, much more, to this ancient story. Besides displaying one man's faith in God in times of suffering, the book of Job has a "missionary" or "missional" purpose. Yet, this facet of Job is rarely addressed.[1]

The Mission of God

In saying the story of Job has a missionary or missional purpose I am arguing that it is connected to what has been referred to as the *missio Dei*, or "mission of God." While this concept has been given a variety of interpretations, basically it means that God is a missionary God and that "mission" is part of God's essential nature and purpose. The "mission of God," then, focuses on God's redemptive purpose and action in human history to heal and restore creation and to call people into a reconciled covenantal relationship with him.[2]

---

1. Walters, "Missio Dei," 19.
2. Van Engen, "'Mission' Defined and Described," 24.

The term *missio Dei* further implies that the many smaller stories in the Bible are in various ways part of a larger "theodrama" or "grand narrative" of redemption which takes place against the backdrop of creation and humanity's fall into sin. It is the "greatest story ever told" that gives the all-embracing perspective for understanding the collection of texts that constitute the canon of Scripture.[3] In the words of Chris Wright:

> That the Old Testament tells a story needs no defense. My point is much greater, however. The Old Testament tells its story as *the* story or, rather, as part of that ultimate and universal story that will ultimately embrace the whole of creation, time, and humanity within its scope. In other words, in reading these texts we are invited to embrace a metanarrative, a grand narrative. . . . It is the story that stretches from Genesis to Revelation, not merely as a good yarn or even as a classic of epic literature, but fundamentally as a *rendering of reality*—an account of the universe we inhabit and of the new creation we are destined for. We live in a storied universe.[4]

A powerful and life-changing aspect of this "grand narrative" is that we are invited to locate ourselves within it and allow it to shape our own identities. This is a key function of the story of Job. For, even as we identify with the struggles of Job to comprehend his suffering we find that the answers he discovers within the context of the "grand narrative" of God's redemptive self-revelation are transformative for us as well. To further understand this we need to explore the relationship between the book of Job and the concept of covenant in the Old Testament.

The Book of Job and the Concept of Covenant

The universal dimensions of God's mission are explicitly described for the first time in God's covenant with Abraham, in which the imperative to "go" is followed by a promise of blessing to Abraham and his progeny (Gen 12:1–3). In this passage as well as on two other occasions (Gen 18:18; 22:18), God promises that all of the nations will be blessed through Abraham.[5] Walter Kaiser describes this as "the formative theology" for a "divine program to glorify himself by bringing salvation to all on planet earth."[6]

---

3. Wright, "*Mission of God*, 64.
4. Ibid., 54–55.
5. For a discussion of these passages see Hesselgrave, *JustMissional Church*, 204–207.
6. Kaiser, *Mission in the Old Testament*, 13.

The Mission of God in the Book of Job

The promise to Abraham is reaffirmed to Moses (Exod 3:6–8; 6:2–8) after the release of the Israelites from their captivity in Egypt. The story of the Israelites and their grumbling, rebellion, and lack of faith despite God's acts of deliverance are well known. As N. T. Wright points out: "The call to them on Sinai spoke of their being God's royal priesthood, a holy nation, his special people, a treasured possessions out of all peoples (Exodus 19:5–6), but a group less like that would be hard to imagine."[7]

There are highpoints, such as God's covenant with David (2 Sam 7:11–17) in which God promises David that an eternal kingdom would come from his offspring or "seed." But, by and large, successive kings of both Israel and Judah fail to live uphold the ideals of the covenant and the Israelites fall into exile for their idolatry, immorality, and refusal to respond to God's call for repentance. Nonetheless, God does not forget his call for Israel to be the people through whom he will redeem the world, humankind, and creation itself. The prophet Isaiah, in particular, emphasizes God's faithfulness to both the covenant and to creation, and his intention to rescue and restore Israel. Isaiah 42:1–4 describes this restoration in terms of the coming of the suffering "Servant of God" who will fulfill the role and mission of Israel and "bring justice to the nations."[8]

The covenant is not explicitly referred to in the book of Job. For that reason, it is generally thought that the covenant is not important to its overall message. However, further analysis strongly suggests that this is not the case and that the concept of covenant is profoundly significant for understanding the message of Job.[9] Although not explicitly mentioned, allusions to the covenant abound.[10] For example, the narrative framework of the book opens with a clear statement of Job's "blamelessness" before God (1:1)—a term that is repeated by God (1:8; 2:3) to describe Job's righteousness and by Job himself (9:20–22) in affirming his own innocence. It is significant that this term is used in other texts to describe Abraham's character (Gen 17:1) and the covenant fidelity that was expected of Israel: "You shall be blameless towards Yahweh your God" (Deut 18:13). There are also strong similarities between the description of Job in chapters 1–2 and the covenant blessings and curses in Deuteronomy 28. The reference to

---

7. Wright, *Evil and the Justice of God*. 56,
8. Ibid., pp. 63–64.
9. Rogland, "The Covenant," 49–62.
10. Ibid. For a more complete discussion of this point the reader is encouraged to read Max Rogland's article.

Job as owning many livestock and having seven sons and seven daughters (both the numbers and their sum being symbols of completeness) points to divine favor and echoes the promises in Deuteronomy to those who are faithful to Yahweh (Deut 28:4, 11). By the same token, the tragedies that Job experiences in the opening chapters of the book are the very same as the curses that Deuteronomy gives for unfaithfulness. The destruction of Job's livestock (1:13–17); the killing of his children (1:18–19); and the painful sores covering his body (2:7)—all are included in the punishments threatened in Deuteronomy for forsaking the Lord (Deut 28:18, 27–35, 51).[11]

Of course, there is a big difference between the cases of the Israelites and Job in that the Israelites were guilty of idolatry and disobedience and rightfully punished as a result while the whole point of the book of Job is that Job was innocent. But, actually, this difference highlights the importance of the covenant context for understanding Job's overall message. Job is conscious of the fact that he has maintained his fundamental covenantal loyalty to God. Therefore, his "complaint" before God takes the form of a legal proceeding. In chapters 28–31 Job gives a final summation of his case before God. He looks back to the time when he experienced all the blessings promised to those who are faithful to the covenant. His description of the time "when my path was drenched with cream and the rock poured out for me streams of olive oil" (29:6) echoes the promise in Deuteronomy that Israel would receive a land filled with springs, wine, olive oil, and honey (Deut 8:6–9). Job had been faithful in practicing the virtues of justice and compassion to the poor, widows, orphans, and foreigners as Deuteronomy instructed (Deut 10:18–19; 15:1–11). But, now he is experiencing the curses of breaking the covenant—public ridicule and scorn, the wasting away of his body, and hostility from God himself. Commenting on these verses, Fyall argues:

> This use of covenant language in Job is important both for the theology of that book and more widely for the theology of covenant . . . It prevents us from understanding covenant in a mechanical way and underlines that covenant is a gift of grace. It shows that while punishment is an inevitable consequence of disobedience, blessing is an act of grace and that suffering will be an inextricable part of the road to that blessing.[12]

---

11. Rogland, "The Covenant," 53–55.
12. Fyall, *Now My Eyes Have Seen You*, 186–87.

A recent event that illustrates this message of Job is the killing of Kayla Mueller, a young Nazarene human rights activist, while being held hostage by ISIS. Kayla dedicated her life to working with Syrian refugees and was taken captive by ISIS militants in August 2013 while leaving a Doctors Without Borders hospital in Aleppo, Syria. According to her mother, a phrase that Kayla often repeated was this: "Some people find God in Church, some people find God in nature, some people find God in love. I find God in suffering."[13] This sharply contrasts with the statement made by one of the characters in M. T. Anderson's book *The Astonishing Life of Octavian Nothing: Traitor to the Nation*:

> Kindness without the promise of profit is an impossibility. You must want something if you are to act. Otherwise, it would be like movement without motivation. Reaction without action. Kinesis without stimulation. Motion without energy. Kindness without profit is like a teapot hovering over a table, held by nothing.[14]

The heart of the book of Job is the question raised by the Accuser before God: "Does Job fear God for nothing?" (1:9a) This is a cynical question that casts doubt on both God's goodness and the genuineness of Job's piety. The following question, "Have you not put a hedge around him?" suggests that God has put a "protective fence" around Job and made it easy for Job to be good. He has secured Job's devotion and goodness by bribery and shielded him from harm.[15] Ultimately, these taunting questions cast doubt on the possibility of a genuine relationship between God and humanity, and ultimately the validity of the covenant itself. Can God be loved for who he is and not just for his gifts? Can we hold on to God and pursue his righteousness when no benefits are attached? Is the covenant between God and humans grounded in genuine faith and love? Or is it based on nothing more than a mechanical system of rewards and punishments? Unfortunately, the Accuser's taunt has a ring of truth to it. In our sinfulness we often tend to be motivated by a desire to curry favor with God and/or others. The message of Job, on the other hand, is that we must trust in God's wisdom rather than a "mechanical tally system" based on a superficial reading of covenantal blessings and curses.[16] Or, as Chris Wright puts it, the "good news" of the book of Job is "that God can be known and trusted,

13. Harris and Holdren, "I find God in Suffering," 1–2.
14. Quoted in Walton, *Job*, 439.
15. Andersen, *Job*, 89.
16. Walton, *Job*, 439.

against all that points in the opposite direction."[17] The gospel implicit in Job lies in the way it confronts "some of the desperate contradictions of life in this fallen world (innocent suffering, loss, the apparent hiddenness of God, futility, unpredictability, death), and still continues to affirm the goodness and sovereignty of the one true living God and to hope in him."[18]

In later chapters I will further develop the argument that Job's suffering is representative of suffering humanity and the travail in creation as a whole. The particularities of Job's plight are wrapped up in the plight of humanity.[19] At the end of the book of Job, God responds to Job's questioning of his just administration of the world. He reminds Job that he alone has power over the Leviathan, the fearsome and mighty creature mentioned throughout as the symbol of evil in the world. This recalls the following passage in Isaiah:

> In that day,
> the Lord will punish with his sword,
> his swift, great and powerful sword,
> Leviathan the gliding serpent;
> Leviathan the coiling serpent;
> he will slay the monster of the sea.
> (Isaiah 27:1)

At this point, it becomes clear that Job's personal story is taken up in "grand narrative" of God's plan for the redemption of his creation. Job himself acknowledges that nothing can thwart God's plan (42:2). The smiting of the Leviathan will lead to the "new creation," which is the final answer to Job's agonies.[20]

Application: The Significance of Job for Us Today

The foregoing discussion raises the question of how the writer of the book of Job is attempting to shape the thinking and conduct of its readers. As a redeemed community and a "people of God" Israel was to reflect God's love, justice, mercy, and holiness to the rest of the world. Of course, the

---

17. Wright, "According to the Scriptures." 15.
18. Ibid.
19. See Davy, "The Book of Job," 188.
20. Fyall, *Now My Eyes Have Seen You*, 171–72.

Israelites often failed in that mission. Nonetheless, the Old Testament books (including Job) were written to show their readers how to live according to their calling and correct them when they failed. In other words, in the book of Job there is a threefold relationship between the story of God's redemptive plan (his mission), Job's story, and the reader's personal story.

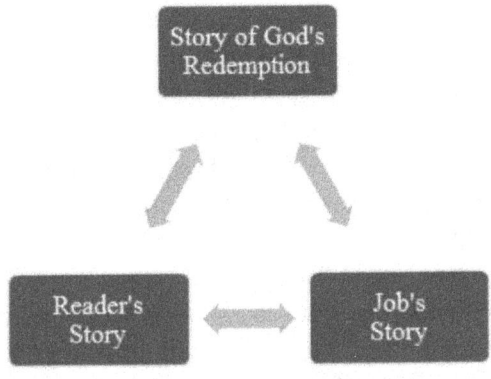

Figure 3 God's Mission, Job's Story, and the Reader's Story

Living by God's Grace and Not by Works

The book of Job is a response to the false theology of the ancient Near East. The common belief was that "there is an exact correspondence between one's behavior and one's destiny."[21] Among Mesopotamians, this belief was associated with a felt need to appease the gods. This appeasement was based on a symbiotic relationship in which the gods had created people to serve their needs and in response to such service protected and provided for the faithful people.[22] Based on this theology, worship of God (or the gods) is based on a *quid pro quo* system of rewards and punishments. God relates to man simply on the basis of his works, either good or bad, not on the basis of grace. I have suggested that this is the essence of the Accuser's attack on God's character and Job's righteousness. Job, he insinuates, expects to "earn" God's favor of material blessing and protection by serving him. Therefore, selfish gain is the foundation of his righteousness rather than a

---

21. Waters, "Missio Dei." 26.
22. Walton, *Job*, 34.

personal intimate relationship with God based on love, trust, and faith in him (1:8–10; 2:3; cf. 1–21–22; 2:10).[23]

Job's friends also strictly adhere to the doctrine of retribution, thereby concluding that Job's suffering must be the punishment for some sin in his life. But, as Richard Rohr says, the "book of Job proclaims from the beginning that there is no [fixed] correlation between sin and suffering, between virtue and reward. That logic is hard for us to break. This book tries to break it, that a new logos called *grace* can happen."[24] It seems that Job is saying that suffering is the path to a deeper understanding and experience of God's love and grace. Suffering (including undeserved and unjust suffering) can also be a means to witness to God's goodness, love, and grace. This message is more fully developed in the New Testament where the apostle Paul calls the church to a life of "cruciform" faith, love, and hope that embodies and bears witness to Jesus' sacrificial love on the cross (Phil 3:10).[25]

An illustration of this truth can be seen in the tragedy that recently gripped the nation involving the slaying of nine African-American worshipers by Dylann Roof, a 21 year-old white supremacist, in a predominately black church in Charleston, South Carolina. One of the most poignant and unforgettable moments occurred in the courtroom where the relatives of the victims stood up and both expressed their grief and offered their forgiveness to the gunman. One said, her voice quivering, "You took something precious from me . . . But God forgives you and I forgive you." Another stated of the victims, "Their legacies will live in love, so hate won't win."[26] Of course, we must be careful not to draw the wrong conclusions. The biblical truth that God by his power and grace brings good out of evil does not in any way neutralize the reality of the evil that is committed or the suffering that it brings. Francis Andersen puts such suffering into proper perspective when he states that, "God (but only God) can actually transform evil into good, so that in retrospect (but only in retrospect) is it seen to have actually been good, without diminishing in the least the awful actuality of the evil it was at the time."[27]

---

23. Waters, "Missio Dei," 24.
24. Rohr, *Job and the Mystery of Suffering*, 33.
25. See Gorman, *Cruciformity*, 364–67.
26. Editorial: "Hate Won't Win," 1.
27. Andersen, *Job*, 71–72.

Walking in God's Ways of Justice and Righteousness

I have suggested in the introduction that it is important to recognize the theme of justice for the poor and vulnerable in Job while, at the same time, not ignoring other types of suffering. In Job the connection between mission and the theme of righteousness and justice is "predicated on the assumption that the people of God are to be engaged in significant ways in issues of poverty and justice and that this engagement is understood as being a profoundly missional activity."[28] This is a theme that is emphasized throughout the Old Testament. The expression "keeping the way of the Lord" or "walking in the way of the Lord" is a favorite metaphor used in the Old Testament to describe Israel's covenantal obligations. An important part of Israel's mission was to be an example to other nations. What is implied in this expression is that there is a fundamental difference or distinction between "YHWH's way" and the ways of other gods or of other nations.[29] But what specifically did it mean to walk in the Lord's way? Among other things, it meant to show justice and mercy towards the "quartet of the vulnerable"—the widows, orphans, the alien, and the poor (Deut 10:17–19; 15:7–11; 27:19; Zach 7:10–11).[30] An important aspect of justice in the Old Testament is that of right relationships—with God and others in family and society. In this sense, justice is closely connected with "shalom" or wholeness, completeness, and harmony for both the individual and the community. It is the restoration of the spiritual, economic, and social well-being which God originally intended before the Fall.[31] Thus, the ethical character of Israel is an important part of its mission. God's election of Israel (beginning with Abraham) is "intended to produce a community committed to ethical reflection of God's character. And God's mission of blessing the nations is predicated on such a community actually existing."[32] Of course, at its heart God's promise of using Israel to "bless the nations" was spiritual and redemptive. It is crucial that we not lose sight of this dimension. But God's redemptive work is social and interpersonal (horizontal) as well as

---

28. Davy, "The Book of Job," 250.

29. Wright, *Mission of God*, 363.

30. In the present day, this concept can be broadened to include the unborn, the homeless, political refugees, many single parents, those who are trafficked, the disabled, and the elderly.

31. Cannon, *Social Justice Handbook*, 24–25.

32. Wright, *Mission of God*, 368.

personal and spiritual (vertical). It involves "restorative justice"—bringing wholeness to a fallen creation.[33]

Timothy Davy points out that there are four ways in which Job responds to injustice toward the poor and vulnerable.[34] First he *acknowledges* that there is a problem. His own experience of innocent suffering and his own predicament further sensitizes him to the suffering of others and the injustices that are committed against them (cf. ch. 24). There is also an implicit acknowledgement that because of rampant violence and oppression the people of Israel have been unfaithful to God and have broken the covenant. Second, in his *laments* he weeps and grieves for the poor and oppressed (30:25). Like many of the prophets, Job struggles with God's apparent unresponsiveness to the cries of the poor and afflicted (21: 7–26; 24:1, 12, and 22). I will discuss the role of lament in Job in greater detail in chapter seven of this study. Third, to prove his point that the innocent suffer (and in his own self-defense), Job *tells the story* of injustice to his interlocutors (24:2–17). Finally, in his final defense of his own righteousness, he explains how he has *intervened* on behalf of the poor and oppressed by rescuing (29:12, 17); providing relief and provision (29:13, 15; 31:16–20); pursing legal justice (29:15–16; 31:21); and giving hope (31:16).

In the final scene in which God responds to Job, the reader is left with the conclusion that while Job may be right in calling on God to maintain his cause, it is only God who has the power to achieve it. Therefore, he is in no position to question God's ways (40:8–10).[35] Job's experience of suffering (both personal and vicarious) therefore has missional significance for us. It suggests that

> facing up to the experience of unattributed suffering, with all the attendant vexation, weakness and confusion, is an inevitable, indeed necessary part of our participation in God's mission. It is this pain that leads us into a more meaningful solidarity with and advocacy on behalf of the suffering. Yet, even while the lament goes on, we also find ourselves as dust and ashes, committing ourselves and others to the wisdom of Yahweh and, therefore, to Yahweh himself.[36]

---

33. For a discussion of the meaning of "blessing" in the OT see Hesselgrave, *The JustMissional Church*, 204–7. For an excellent description of restorative justice in the Bible see Marshall, "Divine Justice as Restorative Justice," 11–19.

34. Davy, "The Book of Job," 254–56.

35. See Andersen, *Job*, 308–9.

36. Davy, "The Book of Job," 256.

Mission, Contextualization, and Suffering

This is not the place to go into an extended discussion of contextualization; however, a few words can be said about this issue in relation to our discussion of suffering and mission in the book of Job. Briefly, if mission is rooted in the "metanarrative" of God's purpose to redeem his creation, then contextualization can be defined as "finding ways to faithfully translate and indwell this story of the renewal of creation in the various cultural contexts of the world."[37] This involves "decoding" culture—learning what is creationally good in culture and what has been distorted by sin—and then communicating the gospel in word and deed in ways that show that it is indeed "good news."[38] This forces us to acknowledge and face the massive reality of all types of suffering in the world—however much we in the West may try to avoid it. It also causes us to probe for answers to two questions: 1) How does deep suffering affect people's perceptions of and response to God? And, 2) how can we speak meaningfully of God in the midst of suffering? The book of Job raises both of these questions for us.

Contextualization further involves the radical step of asking God's Spirit to "transform the narratives that govern our lives" so that we ourselves are empowered to live according to a very different story.[39] This means that there is not simply a contextualization of the message of the gospel. The gospel of God's redemptive love and grace is "lived out" in such a way that our very lives become an apologetic for the gospel to a hurting world. In this, Christians can expect to suffer both *in* and *for* the world—though only temporarily and with the expectation of a future inheritance, to the glory of God (1 Pet 1:4–11). Again, this observation is consistent with the overall message of Job although it is most fully explicated in the New Testament.

---

37. Goheen, *Introducing Christian Mission Today*, 190.
38. Ibid., 291–94.
39. Sine, *New Conspirators*, 227.

PART TWO

Job and Wisdom Literature

IN APPROACHING THE BOOK of Job it is important that we understand it as belonging to the biblical genre known as "wisdom literature." Few people understand this part of the Bible or how it relates to the rest of the Bible. Yet, as Grant Osborne argues: "Genre functions as a valuable link between the text and the reader."[40] Every text is part of a larger group of generically related texts or "genres." By understanding how these ancient genres functioned, the reader is better able to determine the correct "rules" or "guidelines" for understanding the text.[41] To fully understand the book of Job, then, we need to know something of the nature and purpose of wisdom literature as a whole.

The concept of "wisdom" in the Old Testament is difficult to define precisely, and various definitions have been given.[42] Basically, we can say that in the Hebrew Bible wisdom involves the search for principles of human behavior based upon laws of the universe, ponders the nature of human life, and raises questions of ultimate meaning. But, most importantly, what differentiates it from other wisdom literature of the ancient Near East is its radically theocentric nature. Despite the diversity within the wisdom tradition I will show that the book of Job reflects four basic themes which are characteristic of the wisdom thinkers (particularly Proverbs and Ecclesiastes) in general: 1) God's ongoing activity in his creation; 2) the ambigu-

---

40. Osborne, *Hermeneutical Spiral*, 150.
41. Ibid., 150–51.
42. See Schultz, "Unity or Diversity," 271–306.

ity and unpredictability of life; 3) the fear of the Lord in response to his sovereignty; and 4) the sovereign grace of God. As we see how these four themes are played out in the story of Job I will also consider their implications for us as modern readers.

2

God's Ongoing Activity in His Creation

THE WISDOM WRITERS PLACE emphasis on the world and everyday life and on personal insight and experience as it relates to God and others. They stress what might be described as a *creation theology and ethic*—or God's ongoing involvement in and ordering of his creation which is the basis of wisdom. Of particular concern within Israelite theology is the belief that God is a just God who administers justice in the world. This naturally raises the issue of the retribution principle, or the conviction that the righteous are rewarded and the wicked are punished. The question is what role does this principle play in Job and the other wisdom books, particularly Proverbs and Ecclesiastes? Before attempting to answer this question (which will also be addressed in the later chapters), let's first look briefly at how creation theology functions in the wisdom literature.

Creation Theology in Old Testament Wisdom Literature

There are four features of creation theology that are central to properly understanding the book of Job (as well as other wisdom literature). These are that: 1) God's work as Creator is foundational to wisdom; 2) we are completely dependent on God as our Creator; 3) there are common principles of morality and justice that can be discerned by all; and 4) justice is rooted in our common humanity as persons created by God.

God as Creator and Wisdom

The starting point for these writers is that God is the Creator of the world, including humans who are created in his image. Therefore the book of Proverbs declares:

> By wisdom the Lord laid the earth's foundations,
> by understanding he set the heavens in place;
> by his knowledge the deeps were divided,
> and the clouds let drop the dew.
> (Prov 3:19–20)

This affirmation of the Creator God is central to wisdom literature.[1] God creates by wisdom and understanding. Not only does he establish order in the beginning; he goes on maintaining the world's order and restraining forces that oppose it.[2] This picture of God as Creator and Sustainer of creation is particularly evident in God's two speeches to Job out of the whirlwind. In Job 38:4–41 Yahweh challenges Job to a journey through the created world:

> Thus the deity leads Job on a tour of wonderment through the created world, drawing attention to YHWHs own power and providence, and to Job's uninformed and impotent status in comparison. The spotlight is turned on the Creator through the creation, lauding his power to create and sustain.[3]

Our Complete Dependence on God

Another emphasis is that since God is God and we are not, we are completely dependent on him. Derek Kidner observes that Proverbs, for all of its emphasis on common sense, exalts faith in God above human wisdom, prudence, and understanding (3:5–7; 16:3; 19:21).[4] Indeed one of the authors of this book[5] specifically states that the purpose of his maxims is to foster trust above everything else:

---

1. Bullock, "Wisdom, the 'Amen' of Torah," 6.
2. Goldingay, *Theological Diversity and the Authority of the Old Testament*, 217.
3. Bullock, "Wisdom, the 'Amen' of Torah," 8.
4. Kidner, *Proverbs*, 33–34.
5. The book of Proverbs makes it clear that it is the work of a number of authors, several of which are named: Solomon, Agur, and Lemuel. (Ibid., 21)

> So that your trust may be in the Lord,
> I teach you today, even you.
> (Prov 22:10)

The book of Ecclesiastes likewise emphasizes the transience and fragility of life. We are constantly in need of God's sustaining grace, for our only good lies in him. So, it states:

> I know that there is nothing better for men than to be happy and do good while they live. That everyone may eat and drink, and find satisfaction in all his toil—this is the gift of God. (Eccl 3:12–13)

The author Qoheleth is not saying "Eat, drink, and be merry for tomorrow we die!" He is simply saying that even the basic created realities of food, drink, work, and relationships come from the hand of God. We should therefore enjoy and be thankful for life as a gift from God.

Initially, this is also Job's attitude. Despite the anguish of losing his possessions and servants to marauding caravans and most of his family in a mighty wind he affirms, "The Lord gave and the Lord has taken away, may the name of the Lord be praised" (Job 1:21b). In other words, "All things belong to God, absolutely, to be given as a gift, not claim, to be taken back without wrong."[6]

A Common Understanding of Principles of Morality and Justice

Another implication of this creation theology is that despite human sinfulness there is a common morality and sense of justice which can be discerned by all people. Some refer to this as "natural revelation." This belief that there are principles common to humanity is often expressed in terms of "proverbs" which warn and persuade on the basis of experience, prudence, and good or bad consequences. We have these same proverbial sayings in American culture. For example, there is the well-known axiom from Ben Franklin that "early to bed, early to rise makes a man healthy, wealthy, and wise." In other words, hard work pays off! Within Israelite society, however, such proverbs were rooted in a belief in one's accountability to the God of creation. As C. Hassell Bullock observes:

> Basic to the system of thought represented in these books is the assumption that God is working through the human mind and world

---

6. Andersen, *Job*, 93.

of nature. Upon that assumption, wisdom begins with the natural order and launches upon a search for deeper understanding of God who created and controls the world of human existence.[7]

The ethical content of wisdom is therefore based directly on the doctrine of God as Creator of the world. And it is from that vantage point that individuals are required to consider their behavior and its consequences. This is related to the "fear of the Lord," which we will see is a central theme in Job and other wisdom books (cf. Job 1:1; Prov 8:23).

Justice Rooted in Our Common Humanity as God's Creation

The foregoing has implications when it comes to the *motivation* for ethical conduct. This can best be seen by looking at the issue which is commonly addressed in the Old Testament—that of justice and compassion for the poor and needy. Here, a comparison of the historical books (i.e., Exodus, Leviticus, and Deuteronomy) with the wisdom literature is revealing.[8] In the historical books, the main theological and motivational basis for practicing justice is what God has done in redeeming Israel out of Egypt. Because God showed justice and compassion in freeing the Israelites from oppression, the people of Israel should show the same justice and compassion toward the poor and needy in their midst (Exod 23:9; Lev 19:33–36; 25:39–43; Deut 15:12–15).

In wisdom texts, on the other hand, the theological rationale for justice is God's love for his creation. Because we all share one Maker, all are equal before God who shows no partiality. What we do to a fellow human being we therefore do to his or her Maker (Prov 14:31; 17:5; 19:17; 22:2). When Job defends his innocence before his protagonists, then, he appeals to the fact that he has always respected the rights of the poorest in recognition of the fact that all alike are the work of God's hands (Job 31:13–15; cf. 22:5–11; 34:19, 28).

Old Testament Wisdom and the Retribution Principle

A basic principle of wisdom literature is that we live in an orderly universe in which there are physical and moral "laws" of cause and effect. In

---

7. Bullock, *An Introduction to Old Testament Poetic Books*, 62.
8. On this see Wright, *Mission of God*, 449.

the moral realm this means that evil deeds are punished and good deeds are rewarded (Prov 10:30). It is often argued that the traditional wisdom literature of Israel (as represented especially by the book of Proverbs) presented a "fixed order" in which God *always* responds with punishment for wrongdoing and blessing or rewards for good conduct. The unconditional application of this principle of retribution in *all* contexts would mean that a suffering person is uncritically identified as a sinner and a prosperous person as a righteous person. The latter books of Ecclesiastes and Job are then characterized as "wisdom in revolt" in that they are protests against such a rigid "systemization" of the principle of retribution.[9]

However, Walton argues that a distinction must be made between the application of the retribution principle within *Israelite* theology (i.e., theological tradition) and its understanding within the *biblical* theology (i.e., wisdom literature).[10] As a whole, the Israelites (who were influenced by outside religions) tended to accept as true the more rigid and universal application of the retribution principle—that individuals *always* get what they deserve (whether blessing or punishment). From this they also presumed that the one who prospers is righteous and the person who suffers is wicked or guilty of sin. This is the "dogma" which is defended by Job's friends, and which leads them to deny Job's righteousness. But the biblical theology of wisdom literature (which reflects the more correct thinking in the Old Testament) is more cautious and nuanced. All of the wisdom books (including Job and Ecclesiastes) accept the retribution principle as a theological description of God's character—he delights in bringing blessing to those who are faithful and takes seriously the need to punish the sinful. God's restoration of Job at the end of the book is an affirmation of the truth of the retribution principle properly understood as an expression of God's justice, love, and grace. But all of the wisdom books (including Proverbs) also affirm that this principle must be accepted in faith. It cannot be reduced to a rigid philosophical system or fixed formula that is applicable to every situation. God does not operate according to our timetable. Furthermore, the biblical concept of "reward" or "blessing" is often different from our own. Finally, the wisdom books never express the corollary that prosperity equals righteousness and suffering equals wickedness or sinfulness. In this sense, they (and especially Job

---

9. See Roper and Groenewald, "Job and Ecclesiastes," 4–5.
10. Walton, *Job*, 39–45.

and Ecclesiastes) represent a "revolt" against the more dogmatic forms of the retribution principle which characterized Israelite theology.

Application: Job and Joel Osteen

The book of Job raises the fundamental question, "What is my motivation for righteousness and worship of God?" This question is of particular importance in times of trial and suffering. Job's friends hold on to the traditional wisdom that since God is in control of the world and absolutely just there is a fixed and unbroken cause-and-effect relationship between righteousness and blessing and sin and punishment and suffering. Job is therefore counseled that if only he will repent of his sins and become pure and upright, God will restore his prosperity and his life will once again be filled with laughter and shouts of joy (Job 8:6–8; 21). This type of thinking reduces religion to a pragmatic/prosperity formula which is typical of much of the prosperity theology in America today.[11]

The heart of this gospel is the teaching that material prosperity and blessings inevitably flow from the depth and quality of one's faith. Joel Osteen's immensely popular book *Your Best Life Now* promises its readers that if they will follow certain steps they will be happy, healthy, and blessed with everything that makes this life wonderful and fulfilling. In his more recent book *Break Out!* he states:

> When you honor God, when you're good to people, kind, compassionate, and merciful, the blessings will come looking for you. Like the quail, you don't have to go after them. God will shift things to cause the right people to come across your path. God will put you at the right place at the right time so provision, opportunity, comes to you . . . If you will stay faithful and just keep honoring God . . . suddenly things will change, suddenly you come into abundance, suddenly your child straightens up, suddenly you get well.[12]

After giving an example of a faithful church member who was completely healed of a major stroke which had paralyzed the left side of his body and left him unable to walk or talk, Osteen further assures those who may be struggling with sickness, financial problems, or relationship issues:

---

11. Waters, "Reflections on Suffering from the Book of Job," 440–41.
12. Osteen, *Break Out!*, 11.

> God is saying "Yes. A shift is coming. I will shift you out of sickness into health. I will shift you out of lack into abundance. I will shift you out of struggle into ease. I'm about to cross My hands and give you what you do not deserve."[13]

Now, I for one, do not deny that God heals or brings blessing to his people. But, as John Piper reminds us, how we handle loss reveals where our treasure is. Piper puts it well when he states: "The health, wealth, and prosperity 'gospel' swallows up the beauty of Christ in the beauty of his gifts, and turns his gifts into idols."[14] We Americans tend to be motived by self-interest and an attitude of "What's in it for me?" This is fundamentally contrary to the message of Job. Rather, it promotes "disinterested righteousness" as a moral principle.[15] If this is the case, it is natural to ask what this should look like for our faith especially when we go through periods of trial and suffering. How should we discern what God expects of us and what we should expect of ourselves?[16] One of the many problems with the prosperity gospel is that it easily leads either to self-blame and false guilt or to a questioning of God's mercy and goodness when adversity comes. If I suffer, it must mean either that I am somehow at fault or that God is not true to his word. This theology also prevents individuals from understanding and accepting the deeper mysteries of innocent suffering.[17]

As we study this ancient story we need to bear in mind that Job shares with his friends the same belief in the dogma of retribution. The only difference is the conclusions they make based on this principle. In their defense of God's just administration of the world, Job's friends conclude that Job must be guilty of sin. In vigorously defending his own innocence, on the other hand, Job is led to question God's goodness, fairness, and justice. This internal wrestling on the part of Job with Israel's core beliefs is the subject of the next chapter.

---

13. Ibid., 12.
14. Piper, *Don't Waste Your Life*, 72.
15. Walton, *Job*, 275.
16. Ibid.
17. Parsons, "Guidelines," 394.

3

The Ambiguity and Unpredictability of Life

THE SECOND FEATURE OF wisdom literature is an emphasis on the limits of our understanding and our inability to answer all of the questions and problems raised by our experience.[1] Faced with the ambiguity and unpredictability of life, one can only acknowledge the hand of God (Prov 16:9); though, even here, an honest faith may have its doubts. In this chapter I will examine how Job struggles to make sense of the multidimensional nature of his suffering and then draw some practical implications of Job's internal struggle for us today.

Wrestling with Israel's Core Beliefs

The tension between the need for order and faith and an acknowledgement of life's doubts, struggles, pain, and uncertainty is most evident in Job and Ecclesiastes. In particular, these books wrestle with the fact that the retribution principle (that God blesses the righteous and punishes the wicked) often does not square with their own experience. Qoheleth bluntly describes the absurdity of a world where moral values appear to be turned upside down:

> There is something else meaningless that occurs on earth: righteous men who get what the wicked deserve and wicked men who get what the righteous deserve. This too, I say, is meaningless. (Eccl 8:14)

---

1. Goldingay, *Theological Diversity and the Authority of the Old Testament*, 22.

The Ambiguity and Unpredictability of Life

And so, he concludes:

> No one can comprehend what goes on under the sun. Despite all his efforts to search it out, man cannot discover its meaning. Even if a wise man claims he knows, he cannot really comprehend it. (Eccl 8:17)

Chris Wright observes:

> It is hard to avoid the impression that sometimes the sages of Israel held up core Israelite beliefs ("YHWH loves the weak and the poor," "the righteous will be blessed and live, while the wicked will be punished and die") and then throw out the challenge "How can this belief be squared with the real world we live in? Life often simply doesn't follow these rules."[2]

This feature of wisdom literature (which is also found in the Psalms) has been described as "Israel's Counter Testimony," or a cross-examination of Israel's core beliefs regarding God's sovereignty and faithfulness.[3] Again, while I agree with this observation, it must be with the qualifications regarding the retribution principle which were discussed in the previous chapter. I will have more to say about this in chapter five of this study.

The Ambiguity of Life and Suffering in Job

For present purposes, the main question is how this internal wrestling with the issues of life and with core beliefs of the Israelite worldview is reflected in the book of Job. Furthermore, what implications does it have for us as modern readers of this ancient story? To answer these questions we must look at three aspects of Job's suffering: 1) it is innocent; 2) it is affected by unseen cosmic forces; and 3) it is characterized by spiritual and psychological (as well as physical) anguish which precipitates a crisis of faith.

The Reality of Innocent Suffering

We are uncomfortable with suffering, both with the prospect of it happening to us and when it happens to others. Our culture emphasizes the "good life" of comfort, security, and happiness. We work to avoid every possible pain and protect ourselves from misfortune. But Job reminds us of the

2. Wright, *Mission of God*, 451.
3. Ibid.

fragility and uncertainty of life. Job is a wealthy, successful, and powerful man (1:1–3). He has seven sons and three daughters—both numbers and their sum (10) being symbols of wholeness and perfection.[4] To describe Job's life in the modern vernacular, he has it all. Such an idyllic picture leads us to expect that there is more to the story and that things are just too good to be true.[5] Our suspicions are confirmed when, suddenly, everything in Job's world is turned upside down. His property is annihilated and his wealth destroyed; his children are killed along with many of his servants; and his health is taken away (1:13–22; 2:7).

There are two further aspects of Job's suffering which we should bear in mind. First, Job is exposed to multiple traumas. He is portrayed as a victim of both physical tragedy (fire, mighty wind, and painful sores) and the malicious acts by others (raids by Sabeans and Chaldeans). Secondly, Job's suffering is undeserved. The Bible emphasizes Job's goodness to highlight the fact that there is such a thing as innocent suffering.[6] Such pain is made all the more unbearable by the sense that it is totally undeserved, irrational, and therefore unjust. D. A. Carson puts the problem this way:

> Struggle as we may with various facets of the problems of evil and suffering, there are times when particularly virulent evil or horribly inequitable suffering strikes us as staggeringly irrational, unfair. Quite frequently this impression is driven home when we cannot see how to escape the lack of proportion between the massive suffering and the relative inoffensiveness of the afflicted party.[7]

Like Job (and the writer of Ecclesiastes), we may also struggle with the question of why so many good people have a disproportionate number of afflictions and tragedies, while many dishonest, selfish, and greedy people live lives of comfort.[8]

The Cosmic Dimension of Suffering

Kevin Vanhoozer has suggested that the book of Job might be best described as "divine theodrama"—that is, "a series of dramatic scenes, complete with

---

4. Andersen, *Job*, 84.
5. Bartholomew and O'Dowd, *Old Testament Wisdom Literature*. 133.
6. Carson, *How Long, O Lord?*, 140.
7. Ibid., p. 135.
8. Keller, *Walking with God through Pain and Suffering*, 270.

The Ambiguity and Unpredictability of Life

prologue and epilogue that showcase dialogical interaction."[9] The first scene in this ancient "play" opens with the heavenly throne room. The Accuser (literally, "the satan") comes before God, who asks, "Where have you come from?" The Accuser replies, "From roaming through the earth and going back and forth in it (1:6–7). He then charges that the motivation for Job's worship of God is not fear but selfish gain. Suggesting that God has blessed Job to "earn" his praise, he taunts God, "Stretch out your hand and strike everything he has, and he will surely curse your face" (1:11). God then takes the Accuser up on his wager and gives him authority, short of taking his life, to bring destruction on Job (1:12). The Accuser descends to earth with the purpose of destroying every facet of Job's life—his sense of physical and personal well-being, his family and other social relationships, and ultimately his relationship with God. So he incites marauding caravans to kill Job's servants as well as steal and destroy his livestock (1:13–17). The text indicates that the Accuser is also behind the mighty wind that kills Job's sons and daughters (1:18–19). When Job refuses to accuse God of wrongdoing (1:22), the action moves into a second round of dialogue in which God grants the Accuser the authority to afflict Job with painful and unbearable sores over his entire body (2:6).

This section of the book of Job is notoriously difficult to understand. Is it a depiction of what actually happens in the heavenly realms? What are the respective roles of the Accuser (or "the satan") and God in Job's suffering? What is the main purpose of this prologue? These questions are not easily answered. I think Timothy Keller is right when he cautions, "The Bible gives us very little in the way of details about heaven, angels, and the supernatural world, so let's not press the details."[10] Furthermore, "if the purpose of the author was to inform us about such things, he would have given us more specifics."[11] Some scholars further argue that the Accuser depicted in this account is not to be associated with Satan or the devil spoken of later in Scripture.[12] But this much seems clear from reading the book of Job—that we are acted upon by unseen spiritual forces.

Speaking of Job, Vanhoozer observes that "humanity is a veritable cosmic crossroads, a site at which all the powers of the universe converge."[13] The

---

9. Vanhoozer, *Remythologizing Theology*, 345.
10. Keller, *Walking with God through Pain and Suffering*, 272.
11. Ibid.
12. See Walton, *Job*, 65–67; and Bartholomew and O'Dowd, *Old Testament Wisdom Literature*, 134.
13. Vanhoozer, *Remythologizing Theology*, 347.

book of Job (and the Bible in general) brings in three ways of viewing the same event—the human, the divine, and the satanic. All represent different levels of activity and agency.[14] And all are real. There is pain and brokenness in the world because it is fallen. The inclination to use power in a way that causes death and destruction is rooted in human sinfulness. But humans are not alone. It is hard to examine the role of the Accuser in the book of Job (whatever his identity) without being reminded of the depictions of Satan in other parts of the Bible. In the New Testament, Satan is described as the "ruler of the kingdom of the air, the spirit who is now at work in those who are disobedient" (Eph 2:2) and as one who "prowls around like a roaring lion looking for someone to devour" (I Pet 5:8). N. T. Wright is probably correct when he argues that "we have only begun . . . to work seriously at understanding this element, this dimension, in the problem of evil."[15]

However, the book of Job clearly depicts God as the one who is in charge; nothing happens without his permission. Throughout this story God is described as the one who is behind Job's suffering (1:11; 2: 3, 5; 16:9; 19:21; 42:11). This may be difficult for us to understand, much less accept. But, here, some caveats are in order. First, it would be wrong to generalize from Job and characterize all suffering as coming directly from the hand of God. This book is not trying to give us a model of how God is always involved in people's suffering.[16] Second, our understanding of a sovereign God who both brings prosperity and creates disaster (Isa 45:6–7) must be balanced by the love of a God who "does not willingly bring affliction or grief to any human being (Lam 3:33). When we or others we love suffer we must be mindful, then, of the fact that the Bible stresses God's goodness and that he "is never presented as an accomplice of evil, or as secretly malicious, or as standing behind evil in exactly the same way that he stands behind good."[17]

The Spiritual and Psychological Dimensions of Suffering

The further element in this collision between the heavenly and earthly realms is the psychological and emotional dimension of suffering and its possible effect on one's relationship to God. Some have understood the book of Job as an exercise in theodicy, or a response to the question, "Why does God allow

14. Ibid., 348.
15. Wright, *Evil and the Justice of God*, 37–38.
16. Walton, *Job*, 116.
17. Carson, *How Long, O Lord?*, 182.

The Ambiguity and Unpredictability of Life

suffering and evil?" And, in a sense it is, since it addresses God's relationship to his creation. It "raises the question of the moral providence of God in the light of rampant evil—in this case, evil directed at Job himself."[18] But the book is more than a theological defense of God in the face of suffering and evil. It is intensely personal and therefore pastoral. It is important to see that, while the Accuser acts violently against Job, his main purpose is to sow seeds of doubt in God's goodness. Furthermore, Job is never given the reasons for his suffering. He is never permitted to see what has gone on behind the scenes. Such knowledge would have undermined the purpose of his affliction. In Job's mind, his suffering is an unfathomable mystery. Skepticism and fear of the unknown are therefore the major temptations faced by Job, as well as his friends.[19] From a practical or pastoral standpoint, then, the problem of suffering and evil as portrayed in the book of Job is its capacity to cause people to lose their faith in God and to love him in all things and above all things.[20] It introduces the possibility that the sufferer will take the path of Job's wife who cries out, "Curse God and die!" (2:9).

Job's own response shows the difference between thinking about the reality of suffering and actually experiencing it. D. A. Carson notes that Job's statement, "What I feared has come upon me; what I dreaded has happened to me" (3:25) reveals that he had contemplated and probably even dreaded the possibility of disastrous loss. But thinking about it and resolving in advance how you will respond to it cannot prepare you for the shock of suffering itself. "It is like jumping into a bitterly cold lake: you can brace yourself for the experience all day, but when you actually jump in the shock to your system will still snatch your breath away."[21] In the midst of his acute suffering Job enters into an extended and rigorous lament (3:1–26). Job's experience reflects the fact that the initial stage of profound loss is often accompanied by disbelief, fear, anxiety, and confusion which overwhelm one's capacity to cope effectively with the onslaught of unsolicited change. "A reflexive cry of protest expresses itself in an outpouring of emotion. Life as we know it is ripped from our grasp, forcing us to become a reluctant traveler in unfamiliar and frightening territory, with the safe comfort of home only a faraway memory."[22] A bewildering array of questions ("How

---

18. Wright, *Evil and the Justice of God*, 68.
19. Bartholomew and O'Dowd, *Old Testament Wisdom Literature*, 134. See also Carson, *How Long O Lord?*, 141.
20. Swinton, *Raging with Compassion*, 44.
21. Carson, *How Long, O' Lord?*, 141–42.
22. Marr, *The Reluctant Traveler*, 32.

did this happen?" "What will I do now?" "How can I ever be the same?" "Is life even worth living?") lead to feelings of numbness and then growing anger that our most deeply held expectations and beliefs have somehow proven themselves inadequate or false.[23]

Research on the effects of trauma reveals that it calls into question the most basic human relationships. As Judith Herman writes, traumatic events

> breach the attachments of family, friendship, love, and community. They shatter the construction of the self that is formed and sustained in relation to others. They undermine the belief systems that give meaning to human experience. They violate the victim's faith in a natural or divine order and cast the victim into a state of existential crisis.[24]

Traumatized individuals experience damage to those structures which inform their understanding of self. Their self-esteem is attacked by feelings of humiliation, guilt, and helplessness. And they often lose trust in and their sense of connection with themselves, other people, and God. Furthermore, the more severe the trauma, whether measured in terms of the number of people affected or intensity and duration of the harm, the greater the impact.[25] A combat veteran of the Vietnam War describes his loss of faith in this way:

> I could not rationalize in my mind how God let good men die. I had gone to several ... priests. I was sitting there with this one priest and said, "Father, I don't understand this: How does God allow small children to be killed? What is this thing, this war, this bullshit? I got all these friends who are dead." ... That priest, he looked me in the eye and said, "I don't know, son, I've never been in war." I said, "I didn't ask you about war, I asked you about God."[26]

Application: The God Concept and God Image

Job himself never loses his faith in God; but he comes close. In a sense, we might say that Job both experiences and struggles to reconcile the inner dissonance between what he believes about God cognitively or intellectually

---

23. Ibid., 32, 49.
24. Herman, *Trauma and Recovery*, 51.
25. Ibid., 56–57.
26. Ibid., 55.

The Ambiguity and Unpredictability of Life

("God concept") and his experience of God ("God image").[27] The same type of inner conflict is expressed by the psalmist who looks to God for help and comfort in a time of great distress. At one point he expresses confidence in God:

> In you, O Lord, have I taken refuge;
> let me never be put to shame;
> deliver me in your righteousness.
> Turn your ear to me,
> come quickly to my rescue,
> be my rock of refuge,
> a strong fortress to save me.
> Since you are my rock and my fortress,
> for the sake of your name lead and guide me . . .
> Into your hands I commit my spirit;
> redeem me, O Lord, the God of truth.
> (Ps 31:1–3, 5)

But in another Psalm the psalmist expresses doubt about God's willingness to help:

> My God, my God, why have you forsaken me?
> Why are you so far from saving me,
> so far from the words of my groaning?
> O my God, I cry out by day, but you do not answer,
> by night, and am not silent . . .
> But I am but a worm and not a man,
> scorned by men and despised by the people.
> All who see me mock me;
> they hurl insults, shaking their heads,
> (Ps 22:1–2, 6–7)[28]

Both Job and the psalmist exhibit depressive symptoms as they seek to reconcile their experience of God with their faith in God. Glen Moriarty, a clinical psychologist, observes that religious people who are depressed similarly "cognitively understand their faith but do not emotionally understand

---

27. See: Hoffman, Grimes, and Mitchell, "Transcendence, Suffering, and Psychotherapy," 5–7.

28. The contrast between these two Psalms of David is made by H. Newton Maloney in his forward to Moriarty, *Pastoral Care of Depression*, xi.

their faith. They have head knowledge, but not heart knowledge."[29] People who are depressed, even those who are religious and believe in God, will decode, interpret, and internalize information that reinforces negative feelings about themselves, their relationships, and the future.[30] Many whose depression is the result of some severely traumatic experience in their lives such as childhood sexual abuse often feel worthless, unwanted, and literally of no value. This sense of worthlessness affects their understanding of God. They may parrot traditional beliefs (God concept) but have no real experience of God's love (God image). Instead of feeling that they are "fearfully and wonderfully made" (Ps 139:14), they feel that they are a mistake or an accident. Additionally, they are often characterized by guilt, fear of rejection, and perfectionism.[31]

In his suffering Job exhibits many (if not all) of these characteristics of depression. Because he lacks a "God's eye" view of his suffering, he experiences God as distant, angry, and hostile even as he realizes that the only way out of his misery is to trust and hope in this same God. Regardless of whether or not they are clinically depressed, many people can identify with these inner struggles. The world raises some very difficult questions for those who are honest about their own trials and difficulties and the reality of suffering in the world, yet believe in a good, personal, and sovereign God. The book of Job (along with other wisdom writings) "provides a license to think, to wrestle, to struggle, to protest and to argue. All that it asks is that we do so with the undergirding faith and humble commitment encapsulated in its own core testimony that 'the fear of the Lord—that is wisdom, / and to shun evil is understanding.'"[32]

---

29. Ibid., 18.
30. Ibid., 17.
31. Ibid., 18.
32. Wright, *Mission of God*, 452.

4

The Fear of God in Response to His Sovereignty

The "fear of the Lord," says Proverbs, "is the beginning of wisdom" (1:17). This, however, is not a popular concept in our culture; nor is it a topic of many Sunday sermons. As one author has stated, "The contemporary cultural climate has great difficulty in accommodating a positive understanding of the 'fear of the Lord.'"[1] Even in the minds of most Christians, loving God (and the love of God) take precedence over fearing God. In the Bible, however, loving God and fearing him are not opposed; rather, they are two complementary ways of approaching God. This forces us to reconsider our attitudes, even as we read the story of Job. In this chapter I will give an overview of the meaning of the "fear of the Lord" in wisdom literature (including Job) as a whole. A more detailed discussion of this concept as it is used in the book of Job will be reserved for later when we look at the hymn to wisdom in chapter 28.

What is the Fear of the Lord?

In his book *River Out of Eden*, the well-known atheist Richard Dawkins discusses a story in the British newspapers about a bus full of children from a Roman Catholic school that crashed for no obvious reason, with wholesale loss of life. The article went on to quote one priest's response to this tragedy:

---

1. Castelo, "The Fear of the Lord as Theological Method," 150.

The simple answer is that we do not know why there should be a God who lets these awful things happen. But the horror of the crash, to a Christian, confirms the fact that we live in a world of real values: positive and negative. If the universe was just electrons, there would be no problem of evil or suffering.[2]

Dawkins' response as an atheist, however, is that such tragedies are simply the product of blind physical forces:

> Such a universe would be neither evil nor good in intention. It would manifest no intentions of any kind. In a universe of blind physical forces and genetic replication, some people are going to get hurt, other people are going to get lucky, and you won't find any rhyme or reason in it, nor any justice. The universe we observe has precisely the properties we should expect if there is, at bottom, no design, no purpose, no evil and no good, nothing but blind, pitiless indifference. As that unhappy poet A. E. Housman put it:
>
> *For Nature, heartless, witless Nature*
> *Will neither care nor know.*[3]

For Dawkins, the attempt to find spiritual meaning or purpose in the face of suffering is "infantile." The truly "adult" view is that we create our own meaning.[4] But in *The Selfish Gene* he argues that humans are nothing but "survival machines—robot vehicles blindly programmed to preserve the selfish molecules known as genes."[5] If that is true, it is useless to try to teach generosity and altruism.[6] Furthermore, in a strictly materialistic universe suffering has no meaning other than a "chaotic interruption," an accidental interference into the life of the sufferer.[7]

In Proverbs 1:7 there is a contrast between the wise person who fears the Lord and the fool who despises wisdom and instruction. The

---

2. Dawkins, *River Out of Eden*, 132.
3. Ibid., 132–33.
4. Richard Dawkins, *The God Delusion*, 360.
5. In response to Dawkins' argument that we are machines programmed by our genes Anthony Flew comments, "If any of this were true, it would be no use to go on, as Dawkins does, to preach: 'Let us try to teach generosity and altruism, because we are born selfish.' No eloquence can move programmed robots." See Flew, *There is a God*, 80. In chapter ten I briefly discuss the influence of ethics based on materialistic evolution in the rise of Hitler and Nazism in Germany.
6. Ibid.
7. Keller, *Walking with God through Pain and Suffering*, 23.

long prologue of the book (Proverbs 1–9) similarly concludes with the dual affirmation that the fear of the Lord is the beginning of wisdom and knowledge of God brings understanding (9:10). This recalls the words of the psalmist that "the fool says in his heart there is no God" (Ps 14:1). In other words, the wise are wise because they start with God while fools who deny God have no foundation on which to build true wisdom. The starting point for the fear of the Lord, then, is the belief in God's sovereignty and an acknowledgement that he rules over everyone and everything. This is the foundational belief that Job shares with both Proverbs and Ecclesiastes (Job 1:1; Prov 5:21; 16:4; 19:21; 20:24; Eccl 3:10–14).[8]

According to Bullock, the fear of the Lord in wisdom literature has several layers of meaning.[9] The ground layer is an attitude of submission, respect, dependence, and worship before God. It is a basic disposition of true religion. The second layer, which is related to the first, is moral virtue and appropriate behavior. In the opening verses of the book of Job, Job is described as a paragon of virtue who fears the Lord and shuns evil (1:1; cf. Prov 8:13). Ecclesiastes also describes the fear of God in terms of keeping his commandments (Eccl 12:13). The final layer, intertwined with the first and second layers, is an acknowledgement of human weakness and frailty and divine power and strength. At this level, fear of the Lord is equated with complete trust and faith in God (Prov 3:5–7).

Fear of the Lord and Faith in Job and Ecclesiastes

As we have already observed, both Qoheleth and Job wrestle with deep questions of faith. On the one hand, they maintain that the simple moral formula that God always blesses the righteous and always punishes the wicked does not square with human experience. On the other hand, they reject the atheistic answer that life's tragedies prove that God does not exist and that suffering has no meaning or purpose. A superficial reading of Ecclesiastes does leave one with the impression that Qoheleth views life as totally and utterly meaningless. In this book the word translated "vanity" or "meaningless" is repeated thirty-eight times. Many evangelicals interpret this as a description of life apart from a relationship with God. But the word is applied to both believers and unbelievers (7:15; 9:1; 11:8, 10). The key to the book, rather, is found at the very end when Qoheleth concludes that our

8. Smith, "Is There a Place for Job's Wisdom in Old Testament Theology?," 18.
9. Bullock, *An Introduction to Old Testament Poetic Books*, 24–26.

ultimate purpose in life is to fear God and submit in faith to his sovereignty (12:14). As Bullock interprets Ecclesiastes, this is

> the work of a man who had moved through the maze of skepticism and emerged into the freedom of faith . . . He was a man *on the road* to faith, perhaps even a man who had been immersed in faith and then victimized by skepticism, only emerging after a long struggle into a more enlightened faith.[10]

In the case of Job his suffering becomes a test case for whether he fears God under all circumstances of life. The Accuser's challenge to God, "Does Job fear God for no reason?" (1:9, ESV) raises the question of whether Job's basic motivation for righteousness and worship of God is one of love or personal self-aggrandizement. It is a question that Eliphaz throws in Job's face when he chides him, "Is not your fear of God your confidence and the integrity of your ways your hope?"(4:6; ESV). Job's own response is sometimes "yes" (1:20–22; 2:10; 23:10) and at other times, "no" (3:33; 9:22).[11] Only after he has a direct encounter with Yahweh through the whirlwind does Job finally come to an expression of faith which is a perfect illustration of what is means to "fear the Lord" experientially:[12]

> My ears had heard of you
> but now my eyes have seen you.
> Therefore, I despise myself
> and repent in dust in ashes,
> (42:5–6)

Application: G. K. Chesterton's The Man Who Was Thursday and the Book of Job

G. K. Chesterton's classic mystery novel *The Man Who Was Thursday: A Nightmare* is in many ways an allegory on the book of Job. As such, it provides some wonderful and thought- provoking cultural and theological insights into the ancient story. In Chesterton's novel, the main character, Gabriel Syme, is an undercover policeman who is part of a special branch that exists to combat an intellectual conspiracy that threatens civilization.

---

10. Bullock, "Wisdom, the 'Amen' of Torah," 14.
11. Ibid., 16.
12. Ibid.

The Fear of God in Response to His Sovereignty

He is recruited by a mysterious official of Scotland Yard whom he never sees, since he meets him in a pitch-black room. Syme manages to infiltrate an organization of dangerous anarchists and is even able to secure a seat on the Supreme Anarchist Council, which is made up of six members. All of them have code names that are the days of the week. The head of the Council is Sunday; and Syme, the seventh member, becomes Thursday. As the story unfolds, Thursday learns the other five members of the Council (excluding Sunday) are also undercover detectives. Every one of them has been sent on this difficult mission by the same mysterious man whom they have never seen. But as the masks come off, the question arises, "Who is this man called Sunday?" "What is the identity of this man who is the Supreme Head of the anarchists?" At this point, the nightmare begins as each member of the Council tries to catch Sunday. In the end, after a long, arduous, and painful chase, Sunday reveals himself as the mysterious sender, the voice in the dark who made them all detectives. It seems that he has sent them all out on a wild goose chase. But appearances can be deceiving.

What is the point of the story? At one level the story is about six detectives unmasking an anarchist conspiracy; but at another level it is six philosophers trying to figure out what life is all about. Chesterton himself stated that the book is not about the world as it really is; rather it is a depiction of the wild doubt and despair which characterized the pessimists of his day. Sunday represents the "backside of God"—the God behind the events of nature. In describing the "chase," Chesterton seems to be pointing to the absurdity that people often find in life. While we see ample evidence of design and order, we also experience an endless barrage of events that don't seem to have any rhyme or reason. As the detectives struggle to come to grips with Sunday's identity, they waver between awe and bewilderment, fear and anger.[13]

In the final chapter of the book Syme and his companions wrestle with the question of why they had to suffer. Their responses to this question represent different worldviews or philosophies.[14]

Monday is the *intellectually tortured pessimist* who cannot forgive God. When Sunday describes himself as "The Sabbath" and "The Peace of God," Monday responds:

---

13. See West, "The Man Who Was Thursday," 10–11; and Coutts, "A Tale of Emptied Hells," 60.
14. Ibid., 60–75.

Well, I am not reconciled. If you were the man in the dark room, why were you also Sunday, an offense to the sunlight? If you were from the first our father and our friend, why were you also our greatest enemy?[15]

Tuesday is the *anguished man*. His only response is "I wish I knew why I hurt so much."[16]

Wednesday is the *decadent pessimist*. His doubts are used to justify his own quest for power.

Friday represents the *nihilist* who finds life to be meaningless. Good and evil are illusions.

Saturday is the *man of science* who has over-confidence in reason and is blind to the inherent limitations of humanity. In *Orthodoxy*, Chesterton writes of this perspective, "It is the logician who seeks to get the heavens into his head. And it is his head that splits"[17]

The fact is, that there are times when all of us may express one or more of these philosophies. In some respects, they may mirror our own life experience.

Chesterton's unique take on suffering comes at the end of the book. Lucian Gregory, the anarchist, emerges: he is Syme's main protagonist throughout the novel and a figure representing Satan. In a way representative of the Accuser in the book of Job, Gregory charges that Sunday and Thursday are the "good guys" because they have never suffered as he has:

> You are the police—the great fat, smiling men in blue and buttons! You are the Law, and you have never been broken... The unpardonable sin of the supreme power is that it is supreme. I do not curse you for being cruel... I curse you for being safe! You sit in your chairs of stone, and have never come down from them... Oh, I could forgive you everything, you that rule all mankind, if I could feel for once that you had suffered for one hour real agony as I.[18]

At this point Syme has a flash of insight. Responding to Gregory and explaining why he had to suffer, he exclaims:

> So that the real lie of Satan may be flung back in the face of this blasphemer, so that by tears and torture we may earn the right to say

---

15. Chesterton, *The Man Called Thursday*, 274.
16. Ibid., 275.
17. Chesterton, *Orthodoxy*, 29.
18. Chesterton, *The Man Who Was Thursday*, 277–78.

The Fear of God in Response to His Sovereignty

to this man, 'You lie!' No agonies can be too great to buy the right to say to this accuser 'We also have suffered' . . . I repel the slander."[19]

In other words, suffering provides the opportunity for true virtue. Without suffering, we are unproven and untested. Without suffering, all believers are open to the accusation (as was Job) that they loved God and served him merely because they were safe, and for no other reason. By persevering we show Satan himself to be a liar. Philip Yancey puts it well:

> God wants us to choose to love him freely, even when that choice involves pain, because we are committed to him, not to our own good feelings and rewards. He wants us to cleave to him, as Job did, even when we have every reason to deny him hotly.[20]

Facing the frightening prospect of a Sunday who remains aloof, Syme then asks in a dreadful voice: "Have you . . . have you ever suffered?" Sunday's face swells to gigantic proportions and everything goes black. Syme hears what seems to be a distant voice saying a common text he had heard somewhere before: "Can you drink of the cup that I drink of?"[21] With this rhetorical question—an obvious reference to the suffering of Christ—Chesterton's novel comes to an end.

---

19. Ibid., 278.
20. Yancey, *Where is God When It Hurts?*, 91.
21. Chesterton, *The Man Who Was Thursday*, 279.

5

The Redemptive Grace of God

THOSE WHO HAVE STUDIED the wisdom literature have noted the differences between this biblical genre and the historical and prophetic books of the Old Testament. In the latter, the emphasis is placed on the series of historical events through which God reveals his saving purpose. These books emphasize motifs such as the Exodus, God's covenant with Israel, and prophecy. The wisdom books, on the other hand, place more emphasis on daily life and personal experience than on God's unique acts of redemption in history.[1] This is confusing to many Christians who have grown up hearing the gospel of salvation. Zach Eswine describes our usual reaction to wisdom literature in this way:

> Many Christians have grown up traveling the prophetic roads of the Old Testament and the Pauline highways of the New Testament. Wisdom highways are less traveled . . . Job is like a long stretch of desert road with no night light and no gas stations and rest stops for miles. People get stuck out there with no help, so we rarely travel there without a great deal of preparation . . . Ecclesiastes sounds like a crazed man downtown. He smells like he hasn't bathed—looks like it too—and as we pass by he won't stop glaring at us and beckoning to us that our lives are built on illusions, and that we are going to die. So, most of us choose to get our lunch at a different shop on a less dreary corner of town.[2]

---

1. Goldingay, "The 'Salvation History' Perspective," 194.
2. Eswine, *Recovering Eden*, 5.

It needs to be emphasized, however, that while Proverbs, Ecclesiastes, and Job do not explicitly refer to God's covenant relationship with Israel, this is often presupposed. There is more hope, redemption, and divine grace in these wisdom books than is often realized. Yet, this hope of redemption is expressed in relation to a realistic assessment of God and of life in a fallen world. In what follows I will first briefly examine these themes in Proverbs and Ecclesiastes. Then I will further show how the themes of evil, hope, and redemption through God's sovereign grace are developed in the book of Job.

Living Between Proverbs and Ecclesiastes

Within popular Christian thinking there is an often uneasy coexistence of two understandings of the Christian hope. One is a triumphalist Christianity which is reflected in the gospel song "Victory in Jesus." There is, of course, a strong element of truth in this song in that we can and should celebrate and trust in Christ's victory over evil and sin through the Cross. But Christian triumphalism often results in both false optimism and a preoccupation with the individual. It assumes that "I" can live a life free from persecution, suffering, and demonic assault. Since "I" am a child of the King "I" am deserving of financial prosperity and complete physical health. All "I" have to do is follow the right faith "formula." Paul's description of Christians as part of the "groaning" of a fallen creation (Rom 8:22) is foreign to this way of thinking. In the views of some interpreters, the book of Proverbs similarly expresses the same kind of hope (or false optimism) that good will triumph on this earth. If one trusts God and is humble toward him, works hard, is just and loving toward others, that person will be richly blessed and life will go smoothly. This, however, is a one-sided and distorted picture of Proverbs.

The other tendency within Christian thinking is expressed in the words to the hymn, "This World is not My Home." For those who share this perspective, the main purpose for being a Christian is to "go to heaven when I die." As the first stanza of the hymn puts it:

> The angels beckon me from heaven's open door
> and I can't feel at home in this world anymore.

Again, while there is certainly an element of truth in this perspective (I do not wish to deny the importance of scriptural references to heaven!) as

N. T. Wright points out it often leads to the unbiblical conclusion that this created world is at best irrelevant and at worst a dark, evil, gloomy place from which we must escape altogether.[3] For some, this is the picture of the world (minus the references to heaven) that is painted by Ecclesiastes—though, again, I think this is a misrepresentation of its overall message.

A Realistic View of God and Life

A more balanced and correct understanding of Proverbs and Ecclesiastes, I would contend, is to see them as both calling for a realistic view of God and life. On the one hand, we must recognize and face the ugly realities that are part of living in a fallen world. On the other hand, we must affirm faith in God's goodness and his mysterious and providential ordering of all things. These two truths must be held together in creative tension and in such a way that we do not have *either* a one-dimensional and pretentious understanding of God's blessings and our ability to "manage" life *or* an overly simplistic and pessimistic view of life's tragedies. Of course, Proverbs and Ecclesiastes differ in their emphases. One sees the glass as half full while the other sees it as half empty. Put in another way, Proverbs emphasizes the positive side of this dialectic by teaching people how to live before God in everyday life as redeemed creatures. Ecclesiastes, on the other hand, emphasizes the negative side in showing how even the believer who has been the recipient of God's salvation can be plagued by doubts and insecurities.[4] Nonetheless, to use a concept that is more fully and clearly articulated in the New Testament, both wisdom books view God's redemption as both "now" and "not yet."

The Fear of God, Redemption, and Sin

To better understand how this dialectic operates within wisdom literature we need to return to the foundational concept of the "fear of the Lord" which we have noted is equated with our concepts of "reverence for," "commitment and obedience to," and complete "trust in" God. As Kaiser notes, in the wisdom books (as well as the wisdom psalms) "the fear of the Lord" is central to the knowledge and wisdom of God.[5] In Proverbs the "fear of

---

3. Wright, *Surprised by Hope*, 90.
4. Goldingay, *Theological Diversity and the Authority of the Old Testament*, 232–33.
5. Kaiser, "Wisdom Theology," 137.

the Lord" is described as a "fountain of life" (13:14; 14:27) and wisdom and righteousness are called the "tree of life" (3:18; 11:30). These terms denote God's grace-filled sources of renewal, temporal and spiritual.[6] Ecclesiastes likewise links the "fear of God" with the "wholeness of man" (12:13; cf. 3:14; 5:7; 8:12).[7] Despite his doubt and skepticism towards life, he remains convinced that there is "profit" to true wisdom (2:13; 7:11, 12; 10:10).

It is important to realize, however, that the benefits of the "fear of the Lord" are not just for the individual. It has social implications as well. The social outworking of true wisdom among a redeemed people is a society characterized by steadfast love and justice. Therefore, Proverbs echoes the Prophets in asserting that, "To do what is right and just is more acceptable to the Lord than sacrifice" (21:3).[8] However, because of sin we do not experience the fullness of God's blessing, either individually or in our social relationships. As John Goldengay puts it:

> The inherent limitations and pressures of the created order remain; the added bondages of the rebellious order are not wholly overcome. We live as children of two ages, of this age and the age to come, or of this age and the age that is lost.[9]

This is evident in Israel's own story, in which sin is not only manifested as part of the general human condition but is also a consistent feature of its own relationship with God.

It is often assumed that Proverbs presents an overly simplistic and idealized view of life that basically ignores or is blind to the injustices and innocent suffering in the world. Ecclesiastes and Job are therefore viewed as correctives to the naïve theology in Proverbs. However, a more balanced and complete reading of Proverbs reveals that the righteous do suffer unjustly and the wicked do prosper (1:11; 6:17; 17:13, 15; 24:18).[10] In Proverbs, as well as in Ecclesiastes, life in this world is not always fair and godly living does not always pay off "under the sun" (Eccl 3:16; 4:1; 7:15; 9:1).

---

6. Kidner, *Proverbs*, 54. Kidner points out that while most of the references to "life" in Proverbs are to be understood qualitatively, there are two passages (11:7; 14:32) which more firmly point to hope in life beyond the grave (*Proverbs*, 53–56).

7. Kaiser, "Wisdom Theology and the Centre of Old Testament Theology," 140.

8. On the covenantal background to Proverbs, see Kidner, *Proverbs*, 34.

9. Goldingay, *Theological Diversity and the Authority of the Old Testament*, 234.

10. See P. Bricker, "The Doctrine of the 'Two Ways' in Proverbs," 519. Raymond Van Leeuwen likewise observes that "There are many proverbs that assert or imply that the wicked prosper . . . while the innocent suffer." ("Wealth and Poverty," 29.)

The Immanence and Transcendence of God

Also important for understanding redemptive grace in the wisdom literature is the concept of the immanence and transcendence of God. Because God is immanent in the world and is sustaining it by his grace, ordinary human behavior and experience manifest certain "signals of transcendence" which suggest that the ugly realities of life are not the final realities. Even in seemingly the most hopeless situations, humans experience a propensity for hope. It has been observed that even an atheist may sometimes feel grateful for life and the world—except that he has no one to whom he can express his gratitude.[11] Qoheleth gives expression to this hope when he states that God "has made everything beautiful in its time. He has also set eternity in the hearts of men" (3:11). Therefore, even as he gives voice to the empty pursuits, injustices, and painful realities of life, he repeats the theme that "it is good and proper" to enjoy the gifts of work, the love of a spouse, possessions, and food and drink that that have been given by God for us to enjoy (5:18-19; 9:7-10). These tokens of God's grace are a witness to an Eden that once was and has been lost, but will one day be restored in its fullness.[12]

In Proverbs, God's immanence is also expressed in terms of his nearness to people, particularly the helpless and the righteous. God is described as the Defender of the weak and the defenseless (14:31; 15:25; 17:5; 22:2, 22-23; 23:10-11) who rewards those who show grace to the poor (19:17) and holds accountable both those who are indifferent to the needs of the vulnerable (24:11-12) and those who oppress them (23:11). At the end of Ecclesiastes Qoheleth also expresses a confident hope in God's justice:

> For God will bring every deed into judgment,
> including every hidden thing,
> whether it is good or evil.
> (Eccles 12:14; cf. 3:17)

In the world, justice will finally be meted out, though these two wisdom books do not specify either the time or the manner. God's justice does not operate like clockwork or according to our timetable. Presently, the

---

11. Goldingay, *Theological Diversity and the Authority of the Old Testament*, 211.

12. Jack Eswine very effectively discusses this theme in his book *Recovering Eden*. See also Zaspel, "Interview," 1-2.

righteous may live in a topsy-turvy, turbulent world in which the divine order of retribution is seemingly overturned.[13] But God will have the last word.

God's transcendence is expressed in both his rule over all of creation and his incomprehensibility. Ecclesiastes especially emphasizes the folly (literally, "vanity") of trying to domesticate God to human desires and of thinking that we can know what God knows. No one can fathom what God does from beginning to end, or add to or subtract from God's redemptive purposes (3:11, 14). As sovereign Lord, God has hidden almost everything we would like to know about his providential purposes in our lives:

> Consider what God has done:
> Who can straighten what he has made crooked?
> When times are good, be happy;
> but when times are bad, consider:
> God has made the one as well as the other.
> Therefore, a man cannot discover anything about his future.
> (7:13–14)

Proverbs likewise stresses the foolishness of relying upon our own human wisdom apart from trust in God (3:5–6) and holds out little hope for those who lack the guidance and revelation which comes only from God (29:18). Life in and of itself cannot supply the key to the meaning of life. True wisdom comes only from a personal relationship with the God of Israel (Yahweh) who is the source of wisdom. In chapter 8 wisdom functions as the means by which Yahweh created the world.[14] It is identified with God's redemptive purpose which he has established from eternity (8:23; cf. 19:21) and is the only true source of life:

> For whoever finds me finds life
> and receives favor from the Lord.
> But whoever fails to find me harms himself,
> all who hate me love death.
> (8:35–36)

---

13. Waltke, *The Book of Proverbs*, 75–76.
14. Kaiser, "Wisdom Theology," 144.

I Know that My Redeemer Lives

God's Grace and Redemption in the Book of Job

I have given a rather extended treatment of hope, redemption, and divine grace in Proverbs and Ecclesiastes as this wisdom background is essential to understanding how these same themes are expressed in the book of Job. For, despite all the doom and gloom in this story, it is really (as I argued in chapter one) about God's healing, saving, and restorative justice and his intention to bring to completion what he intended for creation in the first place.[15] To show that this is the case, I will briefly discuss the following topics in Job: 1) evil and the created order; 2) the revelation and hiddenness of God; 3) Job's hope for liberation; and 4) the providence and grace of God.

Evil and the Created Order

The story of Job is not just about one individual who experiences personal tragedy. Job shares in the disorder of a creation which is in anguish and longs for its transforming (Rom 8:19–22). This is indicated by the fact the book of Job is filled with images of creation and, at points, even develops something of a "theology" of creation.[16] In chapter 3, for example, Job expresses an almost overwhelming spectacle of human misery.[17] Job curses the day of his birth by exclaiming "May it turn to darkness" (3:3) and "May its morning stars become dark" (3:9). In these verses, Job is using language that is the opposite of Genesis 1:3, 16 which speak of God creating light on the first day by separating it from darkness (vs. 3) and putting the stars in the heavens to give night its identity from dusk to dawn (vs. 16). In the book of Psalms the stars are a sign of God's creative power and goodness and reason for praise and worship (Ps 8:3; 147:4; 148:3). So, Job is basically comparing his misery to an "undoing" of creation—or an unraveling of order and a return to chaos.[18] In the words of Fyall:

> Job's misery here becomes a microcosm of human misery, for to put out the morning stars would not simply be to prevent the day of his birth but the dawning of creation itself . . . At the level of Job's own

---

15. For a discussion of these themes on the book of Job in relation to the Old Testament prophets, see Wright, *Evil and the Justice of God*, 62–74.
16. See Fyall, *Now my Eyes Have Seen You*, 57.
17. Anderson, *Job*, 104.
18. Walton, *Job*, 119.

experience, stars (which would normally be images of hope and joy) become simply a suffocating reminder of his own desolation.[19]

For Job, then, the light which marks the beginning of a new day is a curse, not a blessing. In the same chapter, this curse is further compared to the awakening of Leviathan, or the "monster of the deep" (3:8; cf. 7:12). As Fyall points out, in the Old Testament the raging sea (or "the deep") is associated with the watery chaos that threatens the ordered and good creation, and the "monster of the sea" (often referred to as Leviathan or Behemoth) represents the dark powers of the earth and sea. So, Job is using this imagery to express the reality of cosmic evil that is rooted in creation itself. Job's sorrows are linked with the anguish and suffering that is part of a fallen creation; and Job is at the center of a great cosmic battle raging in the heavenly places.[20]

The Revelation and Hiddenness of God

An important message of the book of Job is that God both reveals and hides himself.[21] We have observed that Job is unaware of the "wager" between God and the Accuser. The events of the heavenly court are concealed from Job though he is acutely aware of the hostile and almost overwhelming presence of evil powers in the universe that threaten his faith. Numerous times throughout his long ordeal he demands a hearing before God; but God's silence is deafening, God seems unwilling to help him and even to communicate with him. Like Qoheleth, Job expresses the seeming purposelessness of life when he complains that he feels "hedged in" by his ignorance and impotence:

> Why is life given to a man
> whose way is hidden
> whom God has hedged in?
> (3:23)

There is a deep irony in Job's choice of words, for the Accuser had previously objected that God had placed a "hedge" of protection around Job (1:10). Job's complaint that his "*way* is hidden" essentially calls into

---

19. Fyall, *Now My Eyes Have Seen You*, 59.
20. Ibid., 83–100,
21. Ibid., 187.

question the promise of Proverbs 3:5–6 that God will direct the paths of those who place their trust in him. Job's experience shows that faith does not eliminate mystery but assumes it.[22] But, after a long wait, God does finally respond to Job (38–41)—thus showing us that the God whose ways are beyond our ways is also the one who reveals himself and brings new depths of insight and understanding.[23] God's self-revelation in the form of a theophany in these chapters is not found elsewhere in wisdom literature. In this respect the book of Job is totally unique. As we will see, this is of particular importance in understanding Job's hymn to wisdom in chapter 28 and its relationship to the rest of the book.

Job's Hope for Liberation

As do the writers of Proverbs and Ecclesiastes, Job does not cease to hope in God's deliverance. This hope is expressed in two remarkable and well-known passages: 13:15 and 19:25–26. In chapter 13 Job fluctuates between hope for personal vindication in God's presence and fear that God might destroy him. This inner tension reaches a high point in verse 15 where he cries out:

> Though he slay me, yet will I hope in him;
> I will surely defend my ways to his face.
> (13:15)

Like some psalms, Job expresses hope in the moral providence of God in the face of rampant evil, in this case evil directed at himself.[24] (See, for example, Psalms 88 and 89.) Despite appearances to the contrary, he refuses to believe that God has totally abandoned him. In 19:25–26, at the height of his suffering and seemingly against all odds this hope is further expressed in the form of a conviction that he will have an advocate or redeemer:

> I know that my Redeemer lives,
> and that in the end he will stand upon the earth.
> And after my skin has been destroyed,
> yet in my flesh I will see God.
> I myself will see him with my own eyes—I, and not another.

---

22. Bartholomew and O'Dowd, *Old Testament Wisdom Literature*, 137–38.
23. Fyall, *Now My Eyes Have Seen You*, 187–88.
24. Wright, *Evil and the Justice of God*, 68.

How my heart yearns within me!
(19:25–27)

Notice the strong emphasis upon "seeing" in this passage. Some argue that Job has in mind a glorious vision after his death. But Andersen maintains, "The references to skin, *flesh* and *eyes* make it clear that Job expects to have this experience as a man, not just a disembodied shade, or in his mind's eye."[25] In the Old Testament, the redeemer (go'el) is a legal and relational term referring to Yahweh as the champion and kinsman of Israel who rescues his people. In Israelite society, the "kinsman redeemer" was the nearest relative who had the obligation to help a family member who was in danger of losing his or her possessions, freedom, or life. So, the context clearly indicates that Job's vindicator is none other than God himself.[26]

This passage is quite amazing since it is expressed in the context of utter rejection—by friends (2–5), society (13–19), and seemingly by God himself (6–12). To this point, many of Job's speeches have grappled with God's goodness, of which he sees little evidence. God has even seemed to him to be an adversary who gnashes his teeth (16:9) and burns in anger against him (19:11). Andersen observes that there are striking parallels here between Job and the suffering servant of Isaiah, through whom God's justice and salvation would be carried out (Isa 53 and 61).[27] It is further significant that Job later compares his plight to that of others who suffer unjustly (24:2–12). He is baffled by God's inaction in the face of social evil (24:1, 12). Yet, he holds out hope that God will ultimately bring down the mighty by his power (24:22–24).

Many commentators see a contradiction between what Job says regarding God's inactivity in 24:1–12 and his affirmation of divine justice and the ultimate fate of the wicked in 24:22–24. But as Alison Lo points out, Job's statements simply reflect the perplexity of his inner life as he strives to reconcile innocent suffering with the goodness of God. Also, they cause the audience to perceive the complexity of real life in his quest for divine justice. The author is also preparing the audience for the Yahweh speeches in which God acknowledges the forces of chaos in the universe as represented by Behemoth (40:15–24) and Leviathan (40:25–41:26). Evil is not dismissed as illusory and wickedness still goes unpunished in God's world.

---

25. Andersen, *Job*, 209.
26. Fyall, *Now My Eyes Have Seen You*, 49.
27. Andersen, *Job*, 208. See also Wright, *Evil and the Justice of God*, 71.

But he is still in control.[28] Considered from within the context of the Bible as a whole, then, Job "shows both the anguish of creation . . . and the hope of liberation from its bondage to decay (Rom 8:19–22)."[29]

The Providence and Grace of God

This brings us to the final message of Job—that in the end evil and suffering do not win; love, mercy, and justice do. In the final scene God restores Job's prosperity and health. Job gains herds twice the size he had before and has seven more sons and three more daughters (42:7–16). For some, this sneaks the prosperity gospel in through the back door. But this misses the point of the book. First, the emphasis is on God's mercy and grace, not some neat mathematical formula which affirms that righteousness always brings prosperity and sin always brings punishment and suffering. "The epilogue simply describes the blessings as the Lord's free gift. The Lord is not nasty or capricious. He may for various reasons withdraw his favor, but his love endures forever."[30] The second and related emphasis is that God's intention is to put things right in his creation. In this sense, the book of Job is consistent with the message of Scripture as a whole, and the anticipation in the New Testament of the New Heavens and the New Earth.[31] But, as N. T. Wright argues, the emphasis of the conclusion

> is about God's moral government of *this* world, not about the way in which we should leave this world behind and find consolation in a different one. We may find the last chapter of the book a little trivial . . . But it insists that if God is the Creator (and that, after all, is the premise of the whole book), then it matters that things be put right within creation itself, not somewhere else."[32]

When God confronts Job in the whirlwind, he asks him over and over what he, Job, knows and understands about the divine works. After this encounter with God, Job exclaims, "I know that that you can do all things; no plan of yours can be thwarted" (42:2). The words "I know" in this passage are the same words that Job used when he expressed his conviction

---

28. Lo, *Job 28 As Rhetoric*, 125–26.
29. Fyall, *Now My Eyes Have Seen You*, 188.
30. Carson, *How Long O Lord?*, 155.
31. Ibid.
32. Wright, *Evil and the Justice of God*, 70–71.

that his "redeemer" (go'el) would vindicate him (19:25). But now Job knows and understands God's providential and redemptive plan for his creation in a new and more powerful way even if the human mind cannot always comprehend the manner of its execution.[33]

Application: Suffering Loves Company but Joy Craves a Crowd[34]

Joni Eareckson Tada tells of her experience in the hospital after breaking her neck in a diving accident. After enduring a long surgery to shave down the bony prominences on her back she was forced for three weeks to lie on what is called a Stryker frame—a long, flat canvas sandwich where she was placed face-up for three hours. Then she had another piece of canvas strapped to her and she was flipped facedown for another three hours. Trapped facedown, staring at the floor hour after hour all she could think was, "Great, God. Way to go. I'm a brand-new Christian. This is the way you treat your new Christians? I'm young in the faith. I prayed for a closer walk with you. If this is your idea of an answer to prayer, I am never going to trust you with another prayer again . . . I hate my existence."[35] Joni describes her bitterness as a "raging torrent." Things got worse when after a week of lying face-down, staring at the floor, she was hit with a bad case of the flu. Suddenly, not being able to move was peanuts compared to not being able to breathe. She states, "I was suffering. I was gasping for breath. I could not move. All was hopeless. All was gone. I was falling backward, head over heels, down for the count, decimated. And I broke. I thought, 'I can't do this, I can't live this way. I would rather die than face this.'"[36]

One day a friend came to see her in the hospital and told her to read Psalm 18. There she read, "In my distress I called to the Lord; I cried to my God for help. From his temple he heard my voice; my cry came before him, into his ears. The earth trembled and quaked . . . He parted the heavens and came down . . . He brought me out into a spacious place; he rescued me"—and here is the best part, she recounts—"because he delighted in me"

---

33. Guttierez, *On Job*, 83–84.
34. Eareckson Tada, "Hope . . . The Best of Things," 191–206.
35. Ibid., 192.
36. Ibid., 193.

(vss. 6–19). Joni states, "Little did I realize that God was parting heaven and earth . . . to reach down and rescue me because he delighted in me."[37]

Joni admits that while desperation is still a part of her life as a quadriplegic, God is using it to chisel away at her self-sufficiency and self-consumption. She tells of how God gave her a new way of looking at her hardship when she visited Thailand as the senior disability representative with the Lausanne Committee for World Evangelization. Among the attendees at the Lausanne conference in Thailand there were thirty-six disability workers from around the world, most of them disabled themselves. One was a tall, beautiful African from Cameroon named Nungu Magdalene Manyi, a polio survivor who has made it her life's ambition to rescue other disabled infants who are left on riverbanks to starve to death because a disability is viewed as a curse or a bad omen by local witch doctors. As she met and worshipped with these other disability representatives, Joni discovered in a new way how when we boast in our affliction and glory in our weaknesses, God's power is poured out on us. Joni herself has started Wheels for the World—a ministry that gives hope to others by delivering wheelchairs and Bibles, and giving the good news and disability training to let people know that cerebral palsy is not a curse from a local witch doctor. Jesus mandates that we go out into the streets and alleys and minister to the poor, the blind, the disabled, and the lame, and help them get busy living, she reminds us, because "misery might love company but joy craves a crowd. And the Father and the Son and the Holy Spirit crave a crowd of joy, joy spilling over and splashing and filling the hearts of thirsty people who are absolutely dehydrated from a lack of hope."[38]

---

37. Ibid., 194.
38. Ibid., 202.

PART THREE

The Speeches in Job

THE THEOLOGICAL THEMES WHICH I have briefly summarized in parts one and two are played out through the speeches which make up the bulk of this ancient theodrama. Initially, there are five protagonists who are all gathered at Job's house: Job's three friends Eliphaz, Bildad, and Zophar, a young man named Elihu, and Job himself. Job's friends are determined to correct Job's theology which he has expressed in an initial lament (3:1–26) with their own theodicy of why he is suffering (4–26). After each of his friends speaks, Job responds. Job's final response (26–27) completely silences his friends. I will argue that the poem to wisdom in chapter 28 is an "interlude" by Job that serves as a transition or pivot between his final response to his friends and the rest of the book. Job's final speech (29–31) is followed by Elihu's speech (31–37). Finally God himself speaks, answering Job out of a storm (38–42).

The structure of the speeches in the book of Job is therefore as follows:

- Chapter 3: Job's opening lament
- Chapters 4–27: Three cycles of speeches between Job and his friends
- Chapter 28: Wisdom Poem
- Chapters 29–31: Job continues his discourse
- Chapters 32–37: Elihu's speech
- Chapters 38–42: The Lord speaks

Keller observes that these speeches taken together contain withering critiques of two common answers to the problem of evil and suffering: 1) the traditional religious moralistic answer that suffering occurs because the sufferer or victim has done something wrong or bad; and 2) the secular nihilistic answer that there is no good reason for why people suffer, and that the existence of suffering proves either that God doesn't exist or that he is cruel.[39]

---

39. Keller, *Walking with God through Pain and Suffering*, 271.

6

Job's Friends

The Moralistic Response to Suffering

THE BULK OF THIS book is taken up with the dialogue between Job and his three friends (4–31). It contains important insights concerning the power of people in the survivor's social world to affect the outcome of the trauma, for good or for ill.[1] The purpose of this chapter is to examine in greater detail the theodicy of Job's friends as an example of a moralistic response to suffering. I will then discuss some common errors we ourselves can be guilty of in even the most well-intentioned efforts to provide comfort and support to those who suffer.

Job's Friends' Theodicy of Suffering

Job's friends sympathize and care deeply about what has happened to him. When they come to his house they barely recognize him; and they begin weeping and tear their clothes. In a further demonstration of compassion and solidarity with Job, they sprinkle their heads with ashes and sit with him for seven days without speaking a word (2:12–13). In this respect, the response of Job's friends is a positive (albeit, from our cultural standpoint, overly dramatic) example of how to respond to persons who are suffering. In the aftermath of traumatic life events, the sense of self can often be

---

1. Herman, *Trauma and Recovery*, 61.

rebuilt only through a positive connection to others. There is need for the assurance of safety and protection. Persons who have been traumatized often simply crave the presence of a sympathetic person.[2] Phil Zylla observes that silence, or the inability to express the depth of one's pain, is often the first stage in a person's response to suffering:

> The first phase of Job's suffering is a period of silence in which the situation is so acute that his friends are speechless, burdened with the weight of Job's distress. The depths of his misery overwhelmed his friends who had come to comfort him and to sympathize with his losses.[3]

But when Job's friends begin speaking (Job 4), things take a dramatic turn. The essence of their theodicy or attempt to explain the reason for Job's suffering is expressed by Eliphaz's question to Job:

> Consider now: who, being innocent, has ever perished?
> Where were the upright ever destroyed?
> As I have observed, those who plow evil and those who sow trouble reap it.
> (4:7–8)

We can surmise that this response of Job's friends to his suffering is well intentioned. They want to speak truth into Job's life. Their advice to Job that his suffering is the result of unconfessed sin in his life is reflected in Old Testament passages which talk about God rewarding the righteous and punishing the proud and evildoers (cf. Isa 3:9–11). This idea of "retributive justice" is in fact the most commonly given explanation for distress and suffering in the Old Testament.[4] Elaine Phillips rightly comments that without this traditional sense of divine justice the whole moral nature of the universe would be upended.[5] So the words of Job's friends contain an important element of truth. But they miss the fact that individual instances of suffering may not be the result of sin. There are a variety of reasons why people suffer. Their counsel is overly simplistic and couched in language that is implicitly condescending and judgmental rather than encouraging

---

2. Ibid.
3. Zyllla, *The Roots of Sorrow*, 81.
4. Ibid., 31.
5 Phillips, "Speaking Truthfully," 31.

and supportive. In the end, they are "miserable comforters" whose advice turns out to be an assault on the already wounded Job.[6]

Avoiding a Moralistic Response to Suffering

The response of Job's friends illustrates how the theodicy of retributive justice and the corresponding doctrine of original sin can be applied moralistically and in a way that directly or indirectly blames even innocent victims for their suffering. Gerald Janzen reminds us that it is often easy for us to dismiss Job's friends as false accusers and to sympathize with Job. But the fact is that if we are honest with ourselves,

> we will acknowledge that we have often interpreted our experience or (more likely) someone else's with some version of the theology of "just deserts," as when we say or think "they had it coming" or "what goes around comes around." If we have not formulated such a theology with their degree of stridency, it may be because we have not found ourselves involved in such an intense and prolonged dialogue as they.[7]

One example of this tendency is the common perception among evangelicals that HIV/AIDS is in large part God's judgment on sin. Unfortunately, such judgments mask the fact that in underdeveloped countries especially a significant percentage of those who suffer from this disease are innocent victims.[8] In Africa, women and teenage girls are disproportionately affected because of the practice of polygamy, the unfaithfulness of husbands, and male exploitation and coercion. There is a burgeoning population of AIDS widows and orphans. AIDS preys most on those who are weak, poor, and vulnerable.

---

6. Capps, "Comfort In Strange Places," 8–9.
7. Janzen, *At the Scent of Water*, 55.
8. See, for example, Carson, *How Long, O Lord?*, 227–33. Carson acknowledges that there are infants born with the disease, hemophiliacs that catch the virus from transfusions, and faithful spouses that are infected by unfaithful spouses. But he argues that the "overwhelming majority" of those who suffer from the disease have engaged in biblically forbidden promiscuity or self-destructive drug use. Therefore, "unlike the plague, the explicit connection between biblically forbidden behavior and contraction of the disease makes it far harder *not* to see the severe hand of God in AIDS" (*How Long, O Lord?*, 231). To his credit, he does not regard this as justifying the withholding of help to those afflicted with AIDS.

We do not know the nature of Job's disease of skin lesions. But it is clear that he not only suffers physically; he is perceived to be unclean.[9] In the eyes of his society he is shunned as an "untouchable." The image of poor Job sitting in a "dung heap" is "reflective of how people throughout the ages have shunned the ill, sick and poor, often to the point of casting them as society's 'untouchables.'"[10] Job's situation is applicable to that of many who suffer from AIDS. Particularly in the developing world, cultural practices combined with religious prejudice and fear (in part stemming from the belief that AIDS is a judgment from God) often makes the plight of these victims even worse. As Chris Wright argues:

> Even if we acknowledge that sexual promiscuity is a major cause of infection, and so some people reap what they sow, there are just far too many people (especially women, children and even the unborn) who have become infected or affected by the disease through no fault or sin of their own for their suffering to be regarded in any sense as God's direct judgment on them . . . Sadly, the opinion that the disease is a direct judgment of God on the sufferer for their own sins, whether externally inflicted or internally accepted, is itself an added ingredient in their isolation and suffering.[11]

Certainly, biblical teaching regarding sexual abstinence and faithfulness in marriage is important in combating this disease. But such teaching must be combined with condemning those cultural and religious practices such as stigmatizing and ostracism, gender prejudice, and oppression which compound the problem.[12]

Application: Some Pitfalls to Avoid in Helping Those Who Suffer

From a practical or pastoral standpoint, then, the account of Job's interaction with his three friends gives us a number of pitfalls that caregivers of various types (pastors, counselors, family, and friends) need to avoid in offering help to those who suffer, particularly those who are innocent victims of severe trauma.

9. Hubble, *Conversation on the Dung Heap*, 7.
10. Ibid., xi.
11. Wright, *Mission of God*, 435.
12. Ibid, 438.

Job's Friends

First, the caregiver should avoid simplistic or pat answers that do not take into consideration the particular situation or circumstance of the sufferer. The use of various theodicies in a way that fails to fully acknowledge the depth of pain and evil and instead attempts to spiritualize away the pain of suffering can have the opposite effect.[13] The story is told of a woman whose 7 year-old daughter died of a brain aneurysm on a Sunday evening while she and her husband were attending a service in their church. During the funeral service, in an attempt to bring some meaning and comfort to the parents, the pastor suggested that God wanted to bring spiritual renewal to members of the church. After stating that God had taken their daughter home to be with the Lord, he went on to say that God's purpose in this tragedy was to cause members of the church to reflect upon the brevity of life and call them to repentance and renewed commitment to the Lord. He then gave an invitation for members to come forward for a prayer of dedication. The suggestion that God caused the death of their daughter to bring about spiritual renewal and repentance in the congregation created a dissonant picture of God's love and, in effect, silenced the pain of the parents. Understandably, the bereaved mother never returned to the church again.[14]

The second pitfall to avoid is unfairly blaming the victim for his or her misfortune. Since they automatically assume that the reason for Job's suffering is some sin in his life, Job's friends attack his righteousness and integrity (cf. 11:2–4); fear of God (vv. 5–6), and morality (vv. 6, 14). Instead of offering support, they put him constantly on the defensive. Job ends up feeling betrayed, alienated, confused, misunderstood, and rejected (6:14–15; 12:5; 19:13–22). His attitude becomes one of hopeless resignation, even to the point of wishing he were dead (10:18–19).

In our own culture, similar difficulties with rigid social judgment are often experienced by rape survivors. "Husbands, lovers, friends, and family all have preconceived notions of what constitutes a rape and how victims ought to respond . . . Many acts that women experience as terrorizing violations may not be regarded as such, even by those closest to them."[15] Conventional social attitudes construe most rapes as consensual sexual relations for which the victims are morally responsible. "Thus women discover an appalling disjunction between their actual experience and the social construction of

---

13. Swinton, *Raging with Compassion*, 19–20.
14. Ibid., 19.
15. Herman, *Trauma and Recovery*, 67.

reality. Women learn that in rape they are not only violated but dishonored."[16] One rape survivor describes her experience in this way:

> It was just so awful that [my mother] didn't believe I had gotten raped. She was sure I had asked for it . . . [My parents] so totally brainwashed me that I wasn't raped that I actually began to doubt it. Or maybe I really wanted it. People said a woman can't get raped if she doesn't want to.[17]

Mental health counselors point out that traumatized people such as war veterans and survivors of domestic and/or sexual violence often blame themselves and struggle to arrive at a realistic balance between unrealistic guilt and denial of moral responsibility. War veterans grapple with images of horror that they have witnessed and have also perpetrated. Especially in the United States, survivors of sex trafficking also often struggle with guilt and shame because of the social stigmas attached to prostitution. At the same time, factors beyond their control such as age, poverty, and histories of family violence greatly increase their vulnerability to commercial sexual exploitation. Drugs are often used to mask the deep pain and shame that they experience. In such situations, both harsh criticism and a naïve dismissal of questions of moral judgment can compound the survivor's self-blame and isolation.[18] Helpers need to listen to the survivor's tale without ascribing blame and help the victim achieve healing in the "broken places."[19]

A final pitfall to be avoided involves the tendency to defend God in a way that silences the suffering person. Job's friends are concerned to defend the justice, holiness, and sovereignty of God. In their thinking, God would be unfair to allow undeserved suffering to come to a righteous man. Therefore, Job's insistence on his innocence is an affront to God's justice and righteousness (8:3, 20).[20] God is so holy and Job is so sinful that the only alternative is for him to humble himself before God and repent. Job's friends' theology does not allow room for any questioning of God. To do so, from their vantage point, would be dishonoring to God. Zylla describes Job's dilemma in this way:

---

16. Ibid.
17. Ibid.
18. Ibid, 66–8.
19. Anderson, *Enhancing Resilience in Survivors of Family Violence*, 123.
20. Waters, "Reflections on Suffering from the Book of Job," 442.

Job's Friends

The tendency to defend God is a natural instinct. We are often like Job's friends who fail to enter into Job's situation . . . It is difficult to muddy the waters with problems that may tarnish God's reputation and sincere believers feel sometimes that it is their responsibility to defend God's honor . . . This was Job's real problem. While his friends were content to leave their theology untested and to defend God's honor, Job wanted an explanation for the reasons of his suffering. He wanted to explore the deeper understanding of God's presence and absence in the midst of his losses, anguish, and suffering. It was crucial to Job that he openly express his grief and learn to articulate the depths of his affliction.[21]

Earlier I mentioned the inner conflict that Job experiences between his God concept (or intellectual understanding of God) and his God image (or experience of God). Frequently, in our culture, the God concept is used to suppress the feelings of abandonment and anger which flow from the God image. This process is reinforced by well-intentioned people in the church. Common phrases which come from our theodicies such as "It was God's will," "She is in a better place now," and "All things work for the good of those that love God" are often used in such a way that they lead to a suppression of any questioning of God's goodness. This protects the "idea of God" (our God concept), but it often leads to even greater feelings of depression, and feelings of being distant from God.[22]

In *Deceived by God?* John Feinberg describes his experience of learning that his wife, Pat, had Huntington's Disease, a progressive neurodegenerative disorder that leads to loss of all voluntary bodily movements, memory loss, depression and various forms of dementia including hallucinations and paranoia. The doctors told him that since the disease is genetically transmitted, each of his children had a 50–50 chance of getting the disease. "In one fell stroke," he writes, "we learned that my whole family was under this cloud of doom."[23] Although he knew intellectually that he had no right to question God, emotionally he felt that God had grievously wronged, even tricked him. Feinberg mentions some of the "unhelpful help" he received during this dark hour. One such unhelpful comment was the advice he received from a colleague that he had to realize that God is bigger than all of our conceptions of him. As a professor of systematic theology who was trained in theology, Feinberg knew that what his colleague said was true. In

---

21. Zylla, *The Roots of Sorrow*, 29.
22. Hoffman, et al., "Transcendence, Suffering, and Psychotherapy," 12.
23. Feinberg, *Deceived By God?*, 28.

essence, his colleague was saying that he had to change his ideas about God. The problem was that this treated a fundamentally emotional problem as an intellectual problem. While the afflicted *may* have a wrong concept of God, if the fundamental religious problem is at root an emotional one that must be handled first.[24] Feinberg relates that his uneasiness increased when he was listening to a Christian radio program. A husband and wife had just lost their daughter, who was in her twenties, in an automobile accident. The couple testified that as a result of this accident several people had come to know the Lord. They concluded that, despite the difficulties and hardship they faced in losing their daughter, it was all for the good. This heightened Feinberg's sense of inadequacy. The implicit message he received was that if he was not experiencing joy in his trial and able to say that his affliction was a good thing, he was not "with it" spiritually.[25] Feinberg later came to experience God's grace in his life and the truth that God can and does bring good out of affliction. But in the earlier stages of his struggles, that was not where he was at emotionally.

Like Job's friends, our inclination in times of suffering is to protect God's image so as not to diminish his sovereignty over us. But psychologists tell us that protection of an ideal God concept through denial and suppression of questions may help people survive through times of crisis and suffering. However, it does not help them grow. True growth and healing can only come if we are honest with our feelings before God.[26] Feinberg states based on his own experience:

> Grief and sorrow in the face of human tragedy are very human emotions. Unless they are admitted and expressed, they will remain inside us and destroy us. Healing cannot come if we deny what we are feeling and act as though it is good that evil has occurred. Those negative feelings must be admitted and expressed. They must be dealt with, not hidden so that the sufferer acts as though everything is all right. We cannot help the afflicted if we expect them to deny their humanness.[27]

It is significant that in the end, while Job's friends thought they were defending God, it is they who are rebuked by God for their folly and wrong theology and it is Job who is vindicated. His friends are even instructed to

---

24. Ibid., 51–2.
25. Ibid., 55–6.
26. Hoffman, et al., "Transcendence, Suffering, and Psychotherapy," 12.
27. Feinberg, *Deceived by God?*, 57.

offer burnt sacrifices for themselves while Job prays for them! (42:7–9). While there are times when Job (wrongly) crosses the line in his questioning of God's justice (38:2), he is still described by God as speaking of him what is right (42:7–8).[28]

---

28. Carson, *How Long, O Lord?*, 147–48.

7

Job's Lament

Honesty before God

THE PREVIOUS CHAPTER INTRODUCED the topic of lament in the book of Job. But it is important to realize that lament is not limited to Job. Over one-third of the Psalms contain laments, complaints, or protests directed toward God and plead to him for help.[1] Almost all of Lamentations consists of lament. It is also found in the Old Testament prophets. As I have already intimated, Christians in the West are not comfortable with lament. This tendency to avoid lament diminishes the Christian experience. Andrew Williams observes:

> Western Christian culture on the whole is not good at voicing the shadows in life. The convention of cheerful piety and reverence has led to a tendency to assume that trust precludes any form of despair and that "lament is unnecessary if one trusts, loves, and obeys God." This risks denying the biblical resource of lament that *enables* one to speak from the reality of suffering, seeking to comprehend the heart of a sovereign God.[2]

In this chapter I will look further at Job's lament and its importance for developing as biblically based response to suffering.

---

1. Williams, "Political Lament and Political Protest," 1.
2. Ibid., 2

Job's Lament

The Characteristics of Lament in Job

Job's lament exhibits a number of characteristics. In particular, it 1) reflects the multidimensional nature of suffering; 2) expresses anguish and perplexity over the extent of injustice in the world; 3) alternates between despair and hope; and 4) presses toward praise of the Almighty. Each of these is important for developing a biblically balanced approach to lament.

Lament and the Multidimensional Nature of Suffering (Job 16–17)

The personal pain that Job feels is multidimensional:[3] First, he experiences excruciating *physical pain* (16: 6, 8 and 13–14). Second, he is in *psychological anguish* (16:20; 17:1, 11, and 15). Third, he faces *social degradation*, or isolation and even scorn from others (16:2–3, 10; 17:2). Finally, spiritually, he feels a deep sense of *abandonment by God* (16:7, 9, 11–12).

Job's experience is not atypical. In fact, a holistic response to suffering requires that friends, family, and caregivers take into account all of these aspects of suffering. "Spiritually truncated responses often fail to take seriously all of the dimensions of suffering or place emphasis on only one of the dimensions to the exclusion of the others."[4] Feinberg relates that in addition to the emotional and physical stress and pain that he and his wife felt after learning of her disease, he also felt abandoned by family and friends. "Invariably when news like this comes, people are very concerned; but because they are afraid that they will say the wrong thing, they tend to stay away. Nobody wants to be like Job's comforters."[5] Though understandable, the physical and emotional withdrawal of others only confirms the worst fears of the person suffering. But worst still, Feinberg felt the absence of God. "And when one knows that God is the only one who can do anything about the problem, it is especially painful to sense his departure."[6] Using contemporary vernacular, Old Testament scholar Chris Wright describes biblical lament in this way: "God, I am hurting; and God, everyone else is laughing. And God, You are not helping very much either; and how long is it going to go on?"[7]

3. Zylla, *The Roots of Sorrow*, 81–84.
4. Ibid., p. 84.
5. Feinberg, *Deceived by God?*, 27.
6. Ibid.
7. Quoted in Fernando, *The Call to Joy and Pain*, 32.

Lament and the Experience of Injustice (Job 24)

In Romans 8 the apostle Paul speaks of the inward "groaning" (vs. 23) that Christians experience in the context of the groaning of the entire creation (vs. 22). This is significant, for it links the personal experience of lament with the larger picture that things are not right in the present arrangement of the world. Life itself isn't right. It is infected by sin and injustice. Job also projects his own experience of pain upon the world of humans generally.[8] In so doing, he connects the feeling that he is suffering unjustly with complaint about injustice in the world. He questions the inactivity of God, who seemingly ignores the cries of the poor and helpless members of society who are exploited by the wicked (24:1–12); and he complains about the high crime rate (24:13–17). He also complains that in this life the wicked who spurn God often prosper and go to their graves in peace (21:7–14). As David Pleins describes Job's frustration, he "sees a topsy-turvy world in which those who are wicked accumulate wealth and live to enjoy it because God does not destroy them."[9] In particular, he is concerned with the method by which the wicked accumulate their wealth—they do so by taking over the land and property of the powerless and exploiting the poor:

> Why does the Almighty not set times for judgment?
> Why must those who know him look in vain for such days?
> Men remove boundary stones;
> they pasture flocks they have stolen.
> They drive away the orphan's donkey
> and take the widow's ox in pledge.
> They thrust the needy from the path
> and force all of the poor of the land into hiding,
> (24:1–4)

This analysis of injustice in Job's laments is strongly reminiscent of the prophetic perspective and also some of the psalms (cf. Ps 109; Jer 12:1–2; Hab 1:1–4, 13). Though (as we have seen) he expresses hope in God's ultimate justice (24:20–24) he (like Habakkuk) cannot understand why injustice often persists without relief (24:1 cf. Hab 1:1–4).[10] Later on, in an extended lament before God, Job looks back to the days before disaster hit.

---

8. Lo, *Job 28 as Rhetoric*, 122.
9. Pleins, *Social Visions of the Hebrew Bible*, 502.
10. Ibid., 505.

In a vigorous defense of his own innocence before God, he makes his own protection of the vulnerable and the disenfranchised the "litmus test" of his own righteousness (29:12–17; 31: 16–23). But apparently it takes personal tragedy in his own life for Job to truly internalize the pain of others and make their anger his own. This, as Gutierrez argues, represents a significant shift in Job's thinking as he moves from his own personal situation of suffering and grief to a broader perspective that includes the sufferings and injustices to which the poor fall victim.[11] In his book the *Wounded Healer*, Henri Nouwen introduces the principle of "shared suffering" as that which gives greater meaning to suffering.[12] We have an increased capacity to compassionately stand with others in their suffering to the extent that we have been there ourselves.

The Alternation between Despair and Hope

A further characteristic of lament in Job is a constant alternation between trust and hope in God and despair, even to the point of accusing God of unfairness. When Job first learns of the death of his sons and daughters, he tears his robes and shaves his head and proclaims, "The Lord gave and the Lord has taken away; may the name of the Lord be praised" (1:21). Even when he is afflicted with sores all over his body he responds to his wife's anger with the rhetorical question, "Shall we accept good from God, and not trouble?" (2:10). Later, however, he curses the day of his birth (3:1). Recognizing that none of this could have happened without God's sanction he complains that he feels trapped, "hedged in" by God (3:23). In chapter 9 Job maintains that he is suffering innocently, yet affirms God's unfathomable justice and power (9:4). Though pleading to God for mercy (9:15), he also accuses God of being unfair and unjust (9:17). In chapter 10 he lashes out at God in anger and bitterness: "Does it please you to oppress me, to spurn the work of your hands, while you smile on the schemes of the wicked?" (10:3). He even suggests that he is caught in some kind of divine scheme to trick him (10:8–17). In still other places Job expresses his hope and trust in God (13:15; 19:25); but in almost the same breath, he cries out that God is out to destroy him and his entire family (15:7–9) and that he has been wronged by God (19:6).

---

11. Gutierrez, *On Job*, 31, 37.
12. Nouwen, *Wounded Healer*, 94–100.

What are we to make of this inner conflict of emotions? First, as we have noted, the book of Job is not unique in this respect. The same pattern of response can be found in the Psalms and other wisdom books. "Lament [generally] ... combines, paradoxically, both uncompromising honesty about evil—including the suspicion that God, because God is sovereign, might be at fault—and trust in that same God."[13] Secondly, our own experiences of pain often contain the same conflicts of emotions. John Feinberg describes how he felt anger towards God after learning of Pat's illness, yet also knew that it was foolish to be angry at the only person who could do something about their bleak situation. Though at times he felt that somehow God had misled him into marrying Pat and raising a family, in the back of his mind he also knew that he had no right to haul God into the courtroom of human moral judgments and put him on trial as though he had done something wrong.[14] He relates how the light came on in his own understanding when he realized that God is not obligated to dole out suffering and blessing to everyone equally on the basis of some sort of egalitarian justice.[15]

Lament and Praise

Our final observation is that lament almost always "presses towards praise" as its ultimate end.[16] This is evident in both the Psalms and Job. Repenting of his limited understanding of God, at the end of his ordeal Job finally exclaims that he has come to know God in a deeper, more intimate way (42:5). But Job does not come to this point of praise until the very end of the book and not without first going through a long period of intense confusion and disorientation. Here, the difference between the books of Job and the Psalms is revealing:

> When you read the Psalms sometimes it appears like a quick road from lament to praise. At times, it looks like the shift occurs in a moment. Job shows us otherwise. The road can be long and grueling. The process is not easy, simple, or quick. At times, the darkness will not relent, the questions go unanswered, the confusion

---

13. Middleton, "Why the 'Greater Good' Isn't a Defense," 2.
14. Feinberg, *Deceived by God?*, 28–29.
15. Ibid., 86–7.
16. Williams, "Biblical Lament and Political Protest," 2.

prevails, and hope remains in exile ... The way of lament is a path that strips us bare in order that we may be clothed.[17]

In the next several chapters we will further explore Job's long and winding path to restoration.

Application: Giving a Voice to Victims of Injustice

Like Job, the book of Nehemiah describes a situation in which poor families lose their land to wealthy creditors because of their inability to pay back loans with excessively high interest rates. Left with no other means of support, some of them are forced to sell their children into slavery (Neh 5:1–5). This account of what happened in the time of Nehemiah is very similar to we see happening today. Human trafficking, which is the modern-day form of slavery, often stems from desperate circumstances created by extreme poverty and political and social corruption. The following is the story of one girl caught in the web of labor trafficking in India:[18]

> In a six-bed women's ward in New Delhi's Safdarjung Hospital lies a frail 15-year-old girl. Her face and head are bandaged, leaving only a bruised blue-black eye and swollen lips. Burn marks and scabs extend down her neck to her whole body, and a disfigured ear clings on to her face like a piece of mangled flesh. A strange stench surrounds her. The nurse who comes to check on her explains the smell. A wound on the girl's skull is rotting and has filled with maggots.
>
> The girl tries to speak. In a muffled voice, she says: "My employer would beat me every day with a broom and a stool. Many times she would put a hot pan on my body and burn my skin. That's how the skin on my skull started peeling out as she repeatedly burned the same spot."

The horrific brutality inflicted on this teenager is not an isolated case. In many rural and deeply impoverished parts of India thousands of underage girls are abducted, lured, or sold by families into prostitution or forced labor. Often, parents who are desperate to make ends meet will sell their daughters to local agents with the false promise that the agent will provide her with a high-paying job. The girls are then resold to traffickers who in turn sell them to brothel owners in major cities or to families for domestic

---

17. Capps, "Comfort in Strange Places," 12.
18. Sur, "Silent Slaves," 1.

labor. Most of these girls are trapped in a vicious cycle of unspeakable violence and intimidation.

Trafficking, of course, is not limited to countries like India. It is a worldwide epidemic, with an estimated 21 million adults and children subjected to forced labor, bonded labor, or forced prostitution.[19] Lacking education and other means of support, most have little knowledge of their rights and no clue of how to escape their desperate circumstances. The mission that I work for as a home-based missionary is currently involved in India and parts of Europe to give a voice to these victims of trafficking by working with other agencies to free them from slavery and provide them with necessary spiritual, emotional, medical, and physical care.

Because trafficking is also a growing problem in the United States, Kathi and I have also been part of forming a ministry for victims of commercial sexual exploitation in the area where we live. Recently, I spoke with a friend of ours who is an employment specialist for the city of Waukegan, Illinois, which is not too far from our home. She described a conversation she had with a 16-year-old girl who had traveled all the way to Waukegan from Texas. As they talked our friend became more and more suspicious that this girl was a trafficking victim. Fearing reprisal from the male who had brought her to the agency and was seated on the other side of the office door, the girl could not say so directly. But my friend could see the fear in her eyes. And so, at the appropriate time she called the authorities, who intervened and made it possible for the girl to return to her family in Texas. This girl was one of thousands of minors in America who are at risk of commercial sexual exploitation.[20] While trafficking can happen anywhere and can take many forms, it is most often tied to situations of poverty, drug addiction, domestic abuse, and gang violence which is endemic in our inner cities.

We are told in Scripture that when Nehemiah heard the report of what was happening in Jerusalem and the ghetto it had become, this well-to-do and powerful cupbearer for the king "sat down and wept" and "mourned, and fasted, and prayed before the God of heaven" (Neh 1:4). By praying in this way, "Nehemiah opened himself up to share in the divine burden, to take on God's heart for the devastated poor, and to participate in what God

---

19. International Labor Office, *Profits and Poverty*, 7.

20. According to the U.S. State Department, 100,000 to 300,000 youth are "at risk" of commercial sexual exploitation annually. But this is only an estimate. Exact numbers are presently unknown.

wanted to do about the fallen city."[21] Robert Linthicum notes that the Latin root for anger is the word "grief." He continues:

> Authentic anger is the process of grieving over the injustice our people are facing, and connecting that injustice with the pain we have experienced in our own lives. All of us have experienced injustice when we were dominated, oppressed or exploited in ways that diminish our sense of self-worth and self-respect . . . Our response may have been rage or tears or frustration or grief, but all of these are simply manifestations of anger.[22]

Nehemiah is able to channel his anger in such a way that it becomes a motivation to earnestly pray for mercy, hope, and restoration for his people. We have seen that while Job's experience of anger is more a crisis of faith, nonetheless his cry is not simply for himself but also for others who experience suffering and injustice. Indeed, the best antidote to grief and anger is to open oneself up to participate in God's plan of transformation.[23] Walter Brueggemann maintains that, biblically, lament cannot be reduced to either the personal/psychological or the political/sociological dimension. Both are important. With the loss of biblical lament we run the risk of unwittingly endorsing a false self (or what he terms "psychological inauthenticity") and endorsing the unjust systems about which no questions can properly be raised.[24] In both cases, when we silence the voice of lament we are particularly likely to silence the most marginalized voices in society.[25]

---

21. Sider, Perkins, Gordon, and Tizon, *Linking Arms, Linking Lives*, 183.
22. Linthicum, *Transforming Power*, 95.
23. Sider, et al., *Linking Arms, Linking Lives*, 184.
24 Brueggemann, "The Costly Loss of Lament," 67.
25. Williams, "Biblical Lament and Political Protest," 3.

8

Where is Wisdom to be Found?

IN THE HYMN TO wisdom in chapter 28 we have what has been referred to as "the most heightened expression of Job's creation theology."[1] It is probably the most discussed section in Job. At the same time, there is little consensus among interpreters as to its meaning and function within this ancient story. There are several observations that help us see the significance of this passage in relation to the flow of the entire book.[2]

First, this wisdom poem is best understood as a speech of Job that follows the collapse of the debate between Job and his friends. As such, it functions as a bridge between the dialogue and the speeches that follow.[3] Chapter 28, then, cannot be viewed in isolation from the surrounding chapters. Rather, it must be interpreted in the context of its relationship to the chapters that come before and after, specifically Job 26–27 and 29–31.

Second, many commentators have observed the calm and contemplative tone of this poem, which contrasts strongly with the turbulence and stridence of Job's debate with his friends. This gives the impression that the poem presents a final resolution to Job's problem. But the emotional outbursts by Job in subsequent passages (29–31) indicate that this is not the case.

Third, the final resolution to Job's problem is found in his direct encounter with Yahweh in 42:1–6 where Job *actualizes* and *internalizes* true wisdom. In other words, final healing comes through Job's firsthand

---

1. Bartholomew and O'Dowd, *Old Testament Wisdom Literature*, 269.
2. The following points are from Lo, *Job 28 as Rhetoric*, 209, 230–32.
3. Ibid., 49.

encounter with God, not through the "secondhand" theologizing that is represented by Job 28. The difference between what Job says in chapter 28 and what he later experiences in his direct encounter with God is characterized in terms of the difference between "hearing" and "seeing:"

> My ears had heard of you
> but now my eyes have seen you
> (42:5)

As has been noted, Job's experience of a theophany is unique in wisdom literature. This *does not* mean that the wisdom expressed in Job 28 is overturned or unimportant. It is still of crucial importance. In fact, much of what this chapter says *points to* and is *in harmony with* the themes found in the Yahweh speeches. In a sense we might say that the wisdom presented in Job 28 is a *way station* on Job's road to recovery although it is not the final destination.

In developing these points I will first look at the collapse of Job's dialogue with his friends (26–27) as a precursor to the wisdom hymn. Then I will more closely examine the wisdom poem in chapter 28. Finally, I will show how Job's complaints in chapters 29–31 are connected to and grow out of 28:28.

The Collapse of the Debate with Job's Friends (Job 26–27)

It has been noted by commentators that the cycles of speeches between Job and his friends become increasingly heated in each subsequent cycle. In the second cycle Job's accusations against God are regarded by his friends as offensive to God's ears and plainly heretical. In the third cycle Eliphaz falsely accuses Job of "great wickedness" (22:5–20). In addition, while the speeches of Job's friends become progressively shorter and shorter, Job's speeches become longer and longer. Chapters 26 and 27 contain some of Job's strongest and most vehement responses to his friend's arguments. They mark the climax in Job's conflict with his friends which results in a total rupture of their dialogue. In effect, "the friends–become–enemies are driven into silence."[4] The debate between Job and his friends comes to an end, so that from then on Job's discourse is directed primarily to God.

In my view, these speeches by Job which lead to the wisdom poem in chapter 28 are significant in two respects for understanding Job's path to

---

4. Ibid.

healing. *First, there is a discrepancy and conflict between what Job knows intellectually and what he experiences emotionally and spiritually.* We have noted throughout this study that Job's experience in suffering is characterized by fluctuations from lament and complaint to trust in God's goodness and wisdom, and back again to protest and complaint.[5] This deep inner conflict comes to a head in Job's final responses to his friends. In chapter 26 Job gives a stirring description of God's hiddenness (26:14) and absolute creative power (26:5–13). He observes that the created order is but a whisper of God's grand design, which is far beyond man's comprehension (vs.14). His friends have used much the same argument to contrast God's majesty and human sinfulness. But Job uses it as powerful rebuttal, in effect turning the table on them: If human understanding is so limited, how can they claim to have a right understanding of Job's situation?[6] In chapter 27 Job then invokes God's judgment on his enemies—which his friends have become.

There is a deep irony in these passages which the narrator wants to communicate to his audience. For, while Job's friends are guilty of twisting the truth to fit their theology, Job's remarks in his self-defense also reveal his own conflicting views of God.[7] Job acknowledges the limits of human wisdom and understanding, yet he is sure that God is treating him unjustly. In his oath he complains that God has denied him justice and embittered his soul (27:2). But by invoking God's judgment on his enemies (which assumes divine justice) he is forced to assert that which he questions. The even larger picture is that these chapters (especially chapter 26) anticipate the structure of the divine speeches in chapters 38–41. So, in the end Yahweh turns the same arguments against Job that he has used against his friends. In sum, Job has difficulty trusting in God's wisdom and justice although he may have some knowledge of it intellectually. This full knowledge will not come until his direct encounter with God.

This brings me to the second observation about Job—and that is that *Job's grievances in his laments spur a movement toward God even when his natural instinct is to move away from God.*[8] Timothy Keller says that this is perhaps the single most practical and concrete thing sufferers can learn from the book of Job.[9] And it is perhaps also the basis for Job's ultimate

---

5. Bartholomew and O'Dowd, *Old Testament Wisdom Literature*, 169.
6. Lo, *Job 28 as Rhetoric*, 164.
7. Ibid., 193–94. The following observations are based on Lo's analysis.
8. Swinton, *Raging with Compassion*, 114.
9. Keller, *Walking with God through Pain and Suffering*, 288.

vindication by God in 42:7–9. Throughout his ordeal Job has doggedly sought the face and presence of God. But this becomes particularly evident with the collapse of his relationship with his friends. For now he has no one else to turn to. Similarly, it is instructive for us

> to acknowledge the corrective impulse to turn to God when our fellow humans let us down. Nowhere is the need for God so great as when all others have rejected and maligned to the point where self-esteem is destroyed.[10]

I would suggest that there are two respects in which Job's relationship to God takes on a new form at this point. First, Job's turn toward God is critical in moving from lament to forgiveness.[11] Job's bitterness reaches a climax in 27:2 where he asserts that "God has made me taste bitterness of soul." This bitterness is not just directed against God. It is also directed against his friends whom he now calls his "enemies" (27:7). The question is this: How can a victim (in this case, Job) express his righteous anger in a way that does not trap him in a vicious cycle of bitterness and hatred? One way is through what John Swinton describes as the "pastoral power" of lamentation which "hands over the experience of evil to God and trusts in God's judgment, mercy, and justice."[12] Job's oath of imprecation against his enemies (vv. 7–10) sounds very much like the imprecatory psalms of David. Many Christians have difficulty with such psalms. How can we view the attitudes expressed by the psalmist as in any way consistent with the teachings on forgiveness which are found elsewhere in the Bible? But, as Swinton argues, such imprecatory prayers have healing power in that they allow the victim to express anger and even rage without resorting to vengeance:

> When you are hurt and broken, very often you want to hurt and hit back. To deny such feelings to self or others is to turn the anger within, which can have devastating psychological effects. The psalmist refuses to keep his anger within . . . His rage is very real, but, if we look a little closer, he is not in fact threatening to avenge his suffering. He is asking God to do so. The imprecatory psalms are ritual prayer. By praying this way, the psalmist is not expressing

---

10. Zylla, *The Roots of Sorrow*, 152.
11. Swinton, *Raging with Compassion*, 131.
12. Ibid., 131.

a desire to take revenge himself. Rather he is giving his very real anger and genuine desire for revenge over to God.[13]

Of course, Job does not achieve full forgiveness and reconciliation with his friends until the epilogue when he is instructed by God to pray for them and offer sacrifices on their behalf (42:8–9). But he is taking steps (albeit small steps) in the right direction.

The second aspect of Job's movement toward God in the wake of the dialogue involves his observation that wisdom is found only in him. This is the central theme of the wisdom poem in chapter 28. As Lo states, "The total collapse of the debate compels Job to probe into the mystery of wisdom and to seek God in person because he knows that his friends cannot help resolve his problem any further. Thus he proceeds to reflect upon the issue of wisdom in Job 28."[14] Of course, as has already been noted, Job does not fully understand the implications of what he asserts; and Job 28 provides only a partial solution to his problem. Nonetheless, what Job says in this chapter is vital.

Job's Wisdom Poem (Job 28)

In some respects it is hard to see how Job 28 could come from the lips of a person whose words elsewhere are so full of pessimism and despair. For this reason, many commentators have attributed this passage to the narrator.[15] However, Job is not a flat, one-dimensional character. His erratic behavior and emotional swings are what we would expect from someone who experiences deep physical, emotional, and spiritual trauma. For this reason, the Job of chapter 28 is not totally out of line with the Job we see elsewhere in this story. In this chapter the main question posed is "Where can wisdom be found? (vv. 12, 20) The main themes of this poem are: 1) the human search for wisdom (1–11); 2) the inaccessibility of wisdom (12–22); and 3) God as the only source of wisdom (23–28).

---

13. Ibid., 173.
14. Lo, *Job 28 as Rhetoric*, 227.
15. Walton, *Job*, 29–30.

Where is Wisdom to be Found?

The human search for wisdom (28:1-11)

Job begins by describing the skill and daring by which miners mine for gold and silver in the darkness of the deepest recesses of the earth (vv. 1–4). Throughout this account, Job's suffering has been consistently linked with images of "darkness" and "the deep" (Leviathan). These images represent the mysterious intersection of creation, cosmic chaos (evil), and suffering (3:4–5, 8–9; 10:21; 24:27).[16] So, at one level this picture of mining is a metaphor for Job's search in the midst of his suffering for the divine wisdom that lies behind creation.[17] At another level (as I have already discussed) Job participates in the anguish of creation which longs for release from its own bondage to corruption (Rom 8:21). In this sense, the image of mining represents the human striving to find and secure something more precious than gold and silver—wisdom.[18] Job describes the human ingenuity and resourcefulness in this effort. Man is unrivaled in bringing the waters and mountains under his control and bringing out hidden treasures (vv. 9– 11).

Although Job's words were composed thousands of years ago, they are so timely that they could have been written yesterday. The modern faith in technological progress is represented by the efforts of some to create a new humanity that reaches for immortality. The World Transhumanist Association has "banded together to put the tools of body and brain to work in pursuit of transcendence and immortality."[19] Among the specific biotechnologies that "transhumanists" embrace for improving the human condition are genetics, stem cell research, cloning, and nanotechnology. They believe that progress made in these areas makes it possible for us to modify human nature so radically that we will become "posthuman." To be posthuman is to reach intellectual heights as far above any current human genius as humans are above other primates; to be resistant to disease and impervious to aging; to have unlimited youth and vigor; to exercise control over their own desires, moods, and mental states; to be able to avoid feeling tired, hateful, or irritated about petty things; to have an increased capacity for pleasure, love, artistic appreciation, and serenity; to experience novel states of consciousness that current human brains cannot access.[20]

---

16. Bartholomew and O'Dowd, *Old Testament Wisdom Literature*, 173.
17. Fyall, *Now My Eyes Have Seen You*, 68–69.
18. Lo, *Job 28 as Rhetoric*, 199.
19. See Eppinette, "Human 2.0," 192.
20. Ibid., 196.

The Inaccessibility of Wisdom (28:12-22)

Job's next point is that human cleverness, knowledge, and ingenuity are not capable of discovering authentic wisdom regarding God, humans, and nature (v. 13). In the human search for knowledge, the spiritual dimension tends to get divorced from wisdom. In this process human wisdom is reduced to mere technique, good behavior, and practical skill which have no rooting in divine wisdom.[21] Moreover, while the human tendency is to regard wisdom as a "commodity" that can be purchased, this is far from the case. Man cannot "buy" wisdom in exchange for the most precious jewels (vv. 15-19). In sum, ultimate wisdom eludes all human attempts to search out and acquire.[22]

Again, Job's words are instructive for us. Movements like transhumanism might seem to represent the views of a radical fringe of our society. However, it is a logical extension of assumptions about technology and the physical world that many, even some Christians, hold.[23] Is it possible that in our own actions and attitudes we are overly optimistic about the value of technology and fail to sufficiently recognize its limits? "It is all too easy to get swept up in the message our culture sells about 'need' for the latest and greatest gadget and forget where our ultimate solution lies."[24]

Wisdom in God Alone (28:23-28)

Job's final point is that true wisdom is found solely in God. Verse 23 emphasizes the absolute contrast between God's knowledge and human understanding. James Wharton puts it well when he states that even if humans could "do the impossible and figure everything out, breaking through to some 'grand unified theory' or 'theory of everything' (as some contemporary physicists dream of doing), we should not yet have approached the ultimate grandeur of God."[25] The poem concludes with the well-known verse:

> And he said to man,
> the fear of the Lord—that is wisdom,

21. Bartholomew and O'Dowd, *Old Testament Wisdom Literature*, 177.
22. Wharton, *Job*, 116.
23. Eppinette, "Human 2.0," p. 106.
24. Ibid.
25. Wharton, *Job*, 116.

and to shun evil is understanding.
(28:28)

This verse is the climax, the "punch line" of the entire chapter. Its meaning is basically the same as what is given in other wisdom literature, particularly Proverbs.

Chapter 28, then, gives a summary of what Job had "heard" all of his life as the answer to life's problems—that wisdom is found in trusting God alone and obeying his commands (cf. Proverbs 28).[26] Fyall's comments on the significance of this chapter are particularly pertinent:

> Chapter 28 is valid as far as it goes. We might characterize it by saying that it is the theologian's answer and as such is no mean theology. However, theology cannot provide the full answer, only an appearance of God himself can, and such an appearance and answer are not theology itself but the reality to which theology points.[27]

Why Me, God? (Job 29-31)

Job's reflection on the meaning of wisdom causes him to think back on what life was like before tragedy hit. He longs for the "good times" of intimate friendship with and blessing from God (29:4), family harmony (v. 5), happiness (v. 6), and social influence and esteem (vv. 7-10). Job emphasizes that his positive reputation stemmed from his practice of the social virtues of compassion and social justice (vv. 12-17; cf. 31:1-37). As Andersen remarks, "For him, right conduct is almost entirely social . . . In Job's conscience, sins are not just wrong things people do, disobeying known laws of God or society; to omit to do good to any fellow human being, of whatever rank or class, would be a grievous offence to God."[28]

This reminiscence by Job of his previous life triggers anger and resentment, for his practice of fearing the Lord and shunning evil has not prevented his suffering. Instead, he is now the laughingstock of even the dregs of society (30:1-10). From his perspective, he is also the object of divine indifference and cruel attacks from God himself (30:20-21). The ultimate

---

26. Lo, *Job 28 as Rhetoric*, 214, 231. I have discussed the meaning of "fear of the Lord" in chapter four.
27. Fyall, *Now My Eyes Have Seen You*, 72-73.
28. Andersen, *Job*, 249.

irony is that while Job wept for those in distress he gets evil in return rather than divine blessings:

> Surely no one lays a hand on a broken man
> when he cries for help in his distress.
> Have I not wept for those in trouble?
> Has not my soul grieved for the poor?
> Yet when I hoped for good, evil came;
> when I looked for light, then came darkness.
> (30:24–26)

In effect, Job is saying, "Why me, God? I've played by the rules, and look where it has gotten me!" Though understandable from a human standpoint, Job's resumption of his protests and complaints reveal that he is still operating according to the traditional dogma of retribution. While on the basis of his own experience he rejects his friend's perspective that virtue invariably leads to happiness he nonetheless shares with them the view that it *ought to*.[29] In one final effort to "force" God's hand, Job ends his lament with a long oath of innocence in which he denies impurity, adultery, failure of hospitality, avarice, idolatry, vindictiveness, and hypocrisy (31:1–40). We will see in the next chapter that this leads Elihu to challenge Job's pride and presumption.

Application: Job and C.S. Lewis

Although C.S. Lewis does not mention the book of Job, the picture he gives in *A Grief Observed* of despair, dissolution, and inner turmoil following the death of his wife from cancer is very similar to that of the ancient poet. While Lewis had reconciled the goodness and love of God with suffering at an intellectual level in *The Problem of Pain*, his autobiographical account in *A Grief Observed* with its searing honesty has a much different tone. At one point, Lewis expresses his deep sense of abandonment by God:

> Meanwhile, where is God? This is one of the most disquieting symptoms. When you are happy, so happy that you have no sense of needing Him, so happy that you are tempted to feel his claims upon you as an interruption, if you remember yourself and turn to Him with gratitude and praise, you will be—or so it feels—welcomed with open arms. But to go to Him when your need is desperate, when all other help is vain, and what do you find? A door

29. Hooks, *Job*, 349.

slammed in your face, and a sound of bolting and double bolting on the inside. After that, silence.[30]

Lewis goes on to question whether God is a loving God or a Cosmic Sadist. And he wonders if his faith was real or imagined. "I thought I trusted in the rope," he writes "until it mattered to me whether it would bear me. Now it matters, and I find I didn't."[31] It is only when Lewis "lets go" of his sorrow that he can begin to receive God's gift of healing. In the *Problem of Pain* Lewis makes the oft-quoted observation that pain is God's "megaphone" to get our attention. But he adds the qualification that though God speaks through the megaphone, his creatures do not have to listen and their responses will be varied based on their individual decisions.[32] In *A Grief Observed* he admits that maybe it was his own sorrow that was stifling the voice of God:

> I have gradually been coming to feel that the door is no longer shut and bolted. Was it my own frantic need that slammed it in my face? . . . Perhaps your own reiterated cries deafen you to the voice you hoped to hear.[33]

Lewis comes to see that unless the sufferer has the capacity to receive, even omnipotence can't give.[34] Similar to Job's experience, this realization marks a turn toward true wisdom.

---

30. Lewis, *A Grief Observed*, 5–6.
31. Ibid., 37.
32. Lewis, *The Problem of Pain*, 93, 95.
33. Lewis, *A Grief Observed*, 46.
34. Ibid.

9

Elihu's Theology

Suffering as an Instrument of God's Redemptive Purpose

ELIHU, WHO BEGINS HIS speeches after Job's dialogue with his friends (Job 32–37), functions more or less as a "legal arbiter." He is angry at Job's friends for wrongly condemning him. He implicitly acknowledges that Job is an innocent sufferer. But he also criticizes Job for wrongly impugning God's character (33:3–4). In fact, the Hebrew meaning of Elihu is "He is my God." How we understand Elihu's speeches is critical to understanding the overall message of the book of Job.

Elihu's Speeches and Practical Theodicy

Elihu's four speeches are characterized by a critical, strident tone which is not that much different from those of Job's elder companions. This has led some interpreters to conclude that he is a young, arrogant "windbag" who misunderstands Job and does not have much wisdom to offer.[1] It is true that Elihu is not always correct in what he says or how he says it. But a more balanced reading of Elihu's speeches interprets them as efforts to expose misconceptions about the nature of God's righteousness and justice

---

1. Postell, "Wineskin or Windbag?," 48–51.

so as to recast suffering as the instrument of God's redemptive purposes.[2] Viewed from this perspective, Elihu's speeches contain some foundational principles for a "practical theodicy" of suffering. A practical theodicy is concerned with the question, "How can human beings continue to love God in the midst of evil and suffering?"[3] It looks for what Swinton calls "gestures of redemption" or practices that resist evil when people are battered by the storms of suffering. It seeks to offer compassionate responses to the sufferer. "However, those responses are always aimed first and foremost at restoring a person to right relationship with God, self, and others."[4]

Ellihu's First Speech (Job 33)

In his first speech (33:8–33) Elihu emphasizes that God often speaks to us in our pain. It seems to Job that God has been silent. Job has been suffering terribly and has cried out to God numerous times, but it seems God gives no answer. Job therefore questions why God is not listening to or responding to his pleas (33:8–13). Elihu's response is that God may well be speaking *through his suffering* in ways that Job does not fully perceive (33:14). In particular, God is using the suffering to chasten Job, preserve him from the sin of pride, and save him from the pit of destructive self-sufficiency (33:19–30). These words are not necessarily new. Earlier Eliphaz interpreted Job's suffering as divine correction and disciplining (5:17–17). But here Elihu's comments do not receive a response from Job.

In the previous chapter, reference was made to the similar argument of C. S. Lewis in the *Problem of Pain* that pain—even the pain and deep misfortunes that fall upon decent, inoffensive, worthy people—is necessary to shatter the illusion that all is well and unmask the delusion of our own self-sufficiency. God knows that our happiness lies only in Him. "Yet we will not seek it in Him as long as He leaves us any other resort where it can even plausibly be looked for."[5] God whispers to us in pleasures, speaks in our consciences, but shouts in our pains. Suffering is therefore God's

---

2. Reitman, *Unlocking Wisdom*, 124.

3. John Swinton argues that this is the primary message that emerges from the book of Job: "The model of resistance [to evil] outlined in the . . . book finds its roots and goal in enabling people to live with Job's questions and to learn what it means to offer Job's response of faith and love." (*Raging with Compassion*, 78–79.)

4. Ibid., 80.

5. Lewis, *The Problem of Pain*, 96.

"megaphone" to arouse a deaf world. "It removes the veil; it plants the flag of truth within the fortress of a rebel soul."[6] Suffering is an invitation to conversion; it is medicinal.[7]

Elihu's Second and Third Speeches (Job 34–35)

In chapters 34 and 35 of Job (Elihu's second and third speeches) the emphasis is on responding to *Job's self-righteous presumption* in questioning God's goodness and justice. It should be kept in mind that Job is a man of faith. At no point in his ordeal does he totally reject his faith in God. But, warns Elihu, in charging God with injustice Job is essentially guilty of the sin of rebellion against the Almighty:

> Job speaks without knowledge;
> his words lack insight.
> Oh, that Job might be tested to the utmost
> for answering like a wicked man!
> To his sin he adds rebellion;
> scornfully he claps his hand among us
> and multiplies his words against God.
>
> (34:35–37)

Here, Elihu's words to Job are clearly lacking in compassion or empathy. Bob Sorge is right in his assessment that Elihu is totally unsympathetic: "He shows how little he understands Job's crucible, and he reveals his lack of compassionate regard for someone else's grief."[8] In this respect, his response to Job's plight, like that of his friends, is less than adequate. But although Job is not guilty of outright rebellion (as Elihu suggests) Elihu is right in warning him that in his affliction Job is being tempted to turn away from God.[9] Later, he cautions Job, "Beware of turning to evil, which you seem to prefer to affliction" (36:21).

Elihu's point is that God has put Job in this situation to show him that as sustainer of the entire universe he alone is sufficient to sustain Job's life

6. Ibid., 93–95.
7. Luevano, *Woman-Killing In Juarez*, 77.
8. Sorge, *Pain, Perplexity, and Promotion*, 55.
9. In this respect, I do not totally agree with Sorge who writes that Elihu "misjudges Job's heart intentions by accusing him of rebellion. In his sincerity, he ends up partnering with the Accuser in condemning Job rather than serving him." (Ibid.)

(34:14). The root of Job's problem is that he has a myopic view of God which diminishes God's greatness and sovereign rule (34:17) and self-righteously presumes that God rewards and punishes on Job's own terms (34:33). God does not listen to the "empty pleas" of people which stem from arrogance and stubborn pride (35:9–13). Much less, then, will God respond to Job when he demands that God give answers according to his timetable and when he charges that God ignores evil (35:14–15). It should be pointed out here that there is often a fine line between honesty before God and prideful presumption. Larry Crabb argues that when Christians respond to God out of self-righteous defiance he will not listen to us.[10] John Feinberg likewise states:

> When there is no affliction in our lives, it is easy to become overly self-sufficient and inattentive to what [God] wants to teach as he desires to draw us closer to himself. When affliction comes, though we may be inclined to rebel against God, if we pay attention to what God is trying to teach us, we may instead learn things we might not have been otherwise open to hear.[11]

Elihu's Fourth Speech (Job 36–37)

In his final speech (36–37) Elihu emphasizes *the mystery and hiddenness of God*. We have seen that while Job makes this same point in his argument with his friends he is guilty of inconsistencies. He and his three friends still implicitly assume that everything in God's universe ought to be explained or understood in terms of human experience and reason. Indeed, it is the nature of all theodicies that, rather than accepting the "unreasonableness of faith," they begin with the assumption that God's ways can be explained and justified by means of some rational criteria.[12] But there are limits to human reason. God, says Elihu, is greater than man (33:12); his greatness is beyond our understanding (36:26) and he does great things that are beyond human comprehension (37:5). In his awesome majesty the Almighty is beyond our reach and exalted in power (37:22–23). There are therefore some things that we will not understand. There will always be mysteries to suffering. God cannot be judged on human terms or his ways reduced to human logic.

---

10. See Reitman, *Unlocking Wisdom*, 139–40, n. 229.
11. Feinberg, *Deceived by God?*, 107.
12. Swinton, *Raging with Compassion*, 42–43.

But this does not mean that God is malicious, capricious, or unpredictable (36:5; 37:25). God is not indifferent to the cries of the poor and the needy (34:28). He does not take his eye off of the righteous (36:7). He brings suffering to chasten the sinner; but he forgives and restores when there is true repentance (36:8–11). Or, to quote a well-known adage, "God comforts the afflicted, and afflicts the comfortable" (cf. Ps 18:27). Elihu reminds Job that when people suffer innocently he speaks to them in their affliction and seeks intimacy with them in their distress. God, he says to Job, "is wooing you from the jaws of distress to a spacious place free from restriction, to the comfort of your table laden with choice food" (36:15–16).[13] If Job will repent of his arrogance and persevere in faith, his affliction could be the basis for greater understanding and drawing closer to God (cf. James 1:1–11).

Application: Virtuous Suffering and a Theology of the Cross

While Elihu's advice to Job has value in developing what I have referred to as a "practical theodicy" of suffering, care must also be taken in applying his theology to specific contexts, especially those involving personal handicaps, disability, and abuse. Critics of Christian theologies of "virtuous suffering" maintain that they foster understandings of abuse, impairment, and disability which encourage passivity, resignation, and acceptance of stigmatization even within the church as appropriate responses of faith and submission to divine testing.[14] The theology of virtuous suffering, it is argued, "has encouraged persons with disabilities to acquiesce to social barriers as a sign of obedience to God and to internalize second-class status inside and outside the church."[15]

At its root, the issue raised by these concerns has to do with the language we use of God in relation to suffering. In what sense can we speak of God as identifying or sympathizing with those who suffer? Is it possible even to speak of a God who suffers with us? Fundamentally, such questions introduce a tension between God's sovereignty (power) and his solidarity (pathos). An overemphasis on God's identification with those who suffer runs the risk of minimizing and even losing his sovereignty. On the other hand, a

---

13. Waters, "Elihu's Theology," 146.
14. Louw, "Virtuous Suffering," 5.
15. Ibid.

theology that emphasizes God's sovereignty incurs the danger of presenting God as distant and alienated from the reality of those who suffer.[16]

Elihu's theology never fully resolves this tension. In fact, as I will argue in greater detail in the conclusion to this study, this tension is only fully resolved in a theology of the cross. For the believer, there can be full submission to God's sovereignty in the knowledge that it is through the cross that God fully demonstrates his love and identifies with persons in their suffering. This theology of the cross is based on Christ's example of sacrificial love. And it reframes our understanding of power (even divine power) in terms of *compassionate empowerment* or power *for* others rather than power *over* others.[17] Or as one survivor of sexual abuse puts it, the relationship between God's power and love is best understood in terms of "fierce tenderness"—an image that locates God's power in the service of God's love.[18] This theology of the cross is of course fully revealed only in the New Testament. But I believe we also see glimpses of it in God's direct response to Job.

---

16. Ibid., 6.
17. Ibid., 8. See also Gorman, *Cruciformity*, 395.
18. See Cook and Guertin, "Childhood Sexual Abuse," 44.

10

The Lord Speaks

Finding Meaning, Security, and Hope in God

A PHENOMENON WHICH INCREASING characterizes American and other Western cultures is what I call "practical atheism." By "practical atheism" I mean the tendency even among those who say they believe in God to live life as if he does not exist. If we are honest with ourselves, even those of us who are Christians can be guilty of practical atheism if we make plans or act as if we must solve our own problems apart from reference to God and his will (James 4:13-17). This condition is often gradual, even imperceptible. And it can occur for a number of reasons. One factor, which I have already mentioned, is an implicit faith in modern technology. This is not to deny that God can and often does use amazing breakthroughs in modern medicine to heal individuals of previously incurable diseases. But when emphasis is placed exclusively, and even primarily, on medicine as a response to suffering, the result often is practical atheism. Another factor is what we may perceive as "unanswered" prayer. Based on letters he has received from individuals who have read his various writings on pain and suffering, Yancey observes that disappointment with God over smaller matters can sow the seeds of doubt. If so many smaller prayers go unanswered, how can I trust God when I'm faced with a major crisis? However, often the root problem is that wrong expectations are placed on God. Yancey writes that he has come to the "profound conviction" that "what we think about God and believe about God matters—*really* matters—as much as anything in life matters."[1] This is evident in the story of Job. The themes emphasized in Elihu's speeches prepare the way for the answer that God himself gives. In this chapter we will see how God directly corrects the misconceptions that Job has about his love, grace, and sovereignty in his life.

Suffering and False Beliefs

Like Job, those who are victimized by (or witness) severe traumas are often tempted to draw wrong conclusions about God from their experience. To those who suffer trauma, John Feinberg offers this advice based on his own experience:

> Though no one's circumstances will be exactly identical to mine, we all need to be reminded how easy it is to build an incorrect case against God through inferential reasoning. Before looking at circumstances and inferring that God has deceived you or done anything else wrong, remember that the conclusion you are drawing may not be the only one possible. It is more likely that you are reading the evidence the wrong way . . . If you look long and hard enough, I am certain you will see that God is not guilty of any wrong-doing.[2]

Another way of putting what Feinberg is saying is that because of their victimization trauma survivors often learn negative or false beliefs about themselves, others, and God. Their core beliefs, including the meaning of their life and negative expectations need to be reframed in light of truth about God.

Those in the helping professions often discount the importance of the spiritual dimension in the healing of survivors and may even perceive organized, dogmatic religion as harmful since various religious precepts have been manipulated and wrongly used by perpetrators to justify social injustice and violence against them. However, there is a growing recognition that the integration of the psychological and spiritual dimensions is essential in three areas: 1) achieving a sense of security; 2) discovering meaning and purpose; and 3) finding hope in suffering.[3] In each of these areas incorporating the spiritual dimension of one's relationship to God is foundational to the healing process. Any pastoral approach to suffering which does not

---

1. Yancey, *Disappointment with God*, 21–26.
2. Feinberg, *Deceived by God?*, 129.
3. Anderson, *Enhancing Resilience in Survivors of Family Violence*, 117–29.

find redemption first and foremost in the reality and healing power of God is fundamentally flawed. This is the primary lesson of Job. In what follows I will argue that through his personal and dramatic encounter with God, Job is able to reconnect his God concept (beliefs about God) with his God image (or experience of God). He discovers that his security, meaning, and hope—the three areas where his experience of suffering is the greatest—are found completely in God himself.

Suffering and God's Mercy and Grace

Throughout his speeches and prayers of lament Job has repeatedly stated his desire to meet God and hear from him directly. At the end of the book Job gets what he asked for, though not in the way that he expected.[4] The Lord answers him out of a storm (38:1). This event is both terrifying and comforting to Job. As one commentator has observed,

> the very *fact* of God's appearance should convince Job that He cares enough about him as Creator to respond to his attempt to find Him—it is the ultimate confirmation of his value as God's agent and should gain his attention to God's redemptive goals, of which Elihu had duly apprised him (33:14–33; 36:5–16).[5]

Timothy Keller adds that there are two features in God's response that indicate that he has not come to judge or crush Job but to reach out to him in grace.[6] First, there is the use of the Hebrew personal name "Yahweh" (translated into English as "the Lord") which has been almost completely absent in the book of Job until now. This is the personal, intimate name that is used in the covenantal, love relationship between God and his people. Secondly, the text states that God *answered* Job out of the storm—which in the Hebrew idiom expresses a dialogue between two parties rather than a one-way communication of an authority to an inferior. So, Job experiences the overwhelming presence of a God who shows himself and allows himself to be seen inasmuch as that is humanly possible.[7] Job's experience might be compared to that of a survivor of trauma who initially feels abandoned by

---

4. Keller, *Walking with God through Pain and Suffering*, 280.
5. Reitman, *Unlocking Wisdom*, 154–55.
6. Keller, *Walking with God through Pain and Suffering*, 281–82.
7. Ibid.

God, but subsequently when looking back on her experience acknowledges that God was there all along. As one survivor of domestic violence put it:

> I always thought God had abandoned me. When I look back, he was right there by my side every step of the way. He put people in my path that He knew I would need to strengthen me, to guide me, before I even did ... I mean it was like divine intervention that me and my daughter got out of our situation.[8]

The Lord as Creator and Sustainer (Job 38–39)

In his first speech to Job, God does not give any reasons for his suffering. But, more importantly, he *does* give the reason for Job's very existence—that he alone is the Creator and Sustainer of the world and all that is in it. This point is made forcefully when God asks Job:

> Where were you when I laid the earth's foundation?
> Tell me, if you understand.
> Who marked off its dimensions?
> Surely you know!"
> (38:4–5)

What follows is a long description of the earth's natural wonders that display God's power and Job's ignorance and lack of understanding. Then, to emphasize the fact that Job's questioning of God's justice is totally unfounded and arrogant in light of his absolute rule, God concludes with a final question:

> Will the one who contends with the Almighty correct him?
> Let him who accuses God answer him!"
> (40:2)

Job can only reply: "I'm unworthy. I'm speechless, I don't have an answer" (40:4–5). This whole exchange, especially the heavy use of irony and sarcasm, underscores the fact that God's knowledge and power far exceed our own. The wonder and mystery of God which cannot be confined to limited human experience must be emphasized. But God's words to Job also contain another message—that if God is so intentional about creating

---

8. Anderson, *Enhancing Resilience in Survivors of Family Violence*, 128.

and sustaining the entire universe how much more will he endeavor to realize his purposes for Job and, by implication, for us as well?[9]

In his account of his "conversion" from atheism, the well-known philosopher Antony Flew points to three questions that led to his "discovery of the Divine:" 1) How did the laws of nature come to be? 2) How did life originate from non-life? And 3) how did the universe come into existence? These three questions, he argues, can only be answered by positing the existence of God or an ultimate "Designer" of the universe. To make his point, he gives the following story:

> Imagine entering a hotel room on your next vacation. The CD player on the bedside table is softly playing a track from your favorite recording. The framed print over the bed is identical to the image that hangs over the fireplace at home. The room is scented with your favorite fragrance. You shake your head in amazement and drop your bags on the floor.
>
> You're suddenly very alert. You step over to the minibar, open the door, and stare in wonder at the contents. Your favorite beverages. Your favorite cookies and candy. Even the brand of bottled water you prefer.
>
> You turn from the minibar, then, gazing around the room, you notice the book on the desk: it's the latest volume by your favorite author. You glance into the bathroom, where personal care and grooming products are lined up on the counter, each one as if it was chosen specifically for you. You switch on the television: it is turned to your favorite channel.
>
> Chances are, with each new discovery about your hospitable new environment, you would be less inclined to think it was all a mere coincidence, right? You might wonder how the hotel managers acquired such detailed information about you. You might marvel at their meticulous preparation. You might even double-check what all this is going to cost you. But you would certainly be inclined to believe that someone knew you were coming.[10]

This vacation scenario, Flew argues, is a "clumsy, limited parallel" to the observation made by many scientists that the laws of nature seem to have been designed or "fine-tuned" in such a way so as to move the universe towards the emergence and sustenance of life. To give one example, it is well known that without proteins life could not exist. An essential step on the road to life is for amino acids to link together to form molecules known

9. Reitman, *Unlocking Wisdom*, 157.
10. Flew, *There is a God*, 113–14.

as peptides. A protein is a long peptide chain known as a polypeptide.[11] The odds against amino acids shuffling at random into the right sequence to form a protein molecule by accident are astronomical—something like one followed by forty thousand zeros. Life as we know it requires hundreds of thousands of specialized proteins.[12] The British Astronomer Fred Hoyle once remarked that the probability of the spontaneous assembly of life might be likened to that of a whirlwind sweeping through a junkyard and producing a fully functioning Boeing 747.[13] This observation has led a number of scientists to conclude that we live in a "bio-friendly" universe. In his book *Vital Dust* the Nobel prize winner Christian de Duve argues that the universe is not a "cosmic joke," but a purposeful entity—"made in such a way as to generate life and mind, bound to give birth to thinking beings able to discern truth, apprehend beauty, feel love, yearn after goodness, define evil, experience mystery."[14] Another physicist, Freeman Dyson, states, "The more I examine the universe and study the details of its architecture the more evidence I find that the universe in some sense knew we were coming."[15] As if to anticipate these observations made by modern physicists regarding the laws of nature, God says to Job:

> Do you know the laws of the heavens?
> Can you set up God's dominion over the earth?
> (38:33)

Job's encounter with God is especially applicable to those who struggle to find meaning in the midst of their suffering. Even therapists who are not necessarily Christian have observed that clients often feel despair, not because of their suffering per se but because of the inability to find meaning or a larger purpose in their suffering. Connecting to a God who is transcendent yet also intimately involved in sustaining his creation is important in helping survivors of trauma to resolve this issue. Just as there is a purpose for life, there is also a purpose for suffering. Kim Anderson (a therapist who is not a Christian but advocates integrating spirituality into trauma practice) has suggested that the following non-confrontational and religiously

---

11. Davies, *The 5th Miracle*, 89.
12. Ibid., 95.
13. Ibid.
14. Ibid., 263.
15. Quoted in Flew, *There is a God*, 114.

neutral questions can be useful in beginning to addressing the "why" of suffering:[16]

- What sustains you? What keeps you going in troubling times?
- Have you ever felt connected to something/someone beyond yourself? How does this connection give you a sense of meaning and/or purpose in life?
- How, if any, have you found meaning in your suffering?
- How, if any, does your suffering provide you with a greater life purpose (e.g., breaking the cycle of violence, wanting to make a difference for others)?

God's Rule Over Evil (Job 40–41)

In his second speech (40:6—41:34) God emphasizes his all-powerful rule over evil. Again, while he does not give the reason for Job's suffering he does address Job's accusations against his moral governance of the world:

> Would you discredit my justice?
> Would you condemn me to justify yourself?
> Do you have an arm like God's and can your voice thunder like his?
> Then adorn yourself with glory and splendor,
> and clothe yourself in honor and majesty.
> Unleash the fury of your wrath,
> look at every proud man and bring him low,
> look at every proud man and humble him,
> crush the wicked where they stand.
> Bury them all in the dust together;
> shroud their faces in the grave.
> Then I myself will admit to you
> that your own right hand can save you.
> (40:8–14)

Central to the book of Job is the conflict between Job's integrity and God's integrity.[17] In defense of his integrity, God challenges Job's assumption

---

16. Anderson, *Enhancing Resilience in Survivors of Family Violence*, 129.
17. Lo, *Job 28 as Rhetoric*, 234.

that he can rule the universe better than God can. "In order to justifiably discredit God's justice yet still deliver himself from affliction (40:14), Job must himself be able to subdue and control all the evil forces sustaining his affliction."[18] But Job is powerless over the forces of evil, which are represented by Behemoth and Leviathan (40:15–41:10). Since Job has no hope of subduing these powerful forces, he must drop his charges against God who alone has power over evil and to whom the whole universe belongs (41:8–11).[19]

Fyall points out that, theologically, there are two emphases in God's final speech. The first is the fearsome reality of evil that is linked with creation. "Creation itself has violence as well as beauty and is shot through with pain and distress."[20] But the second emphasis is that Leviathan is but a creature that is not beyond divine providence and control:

> Who has a claim against me that I must pay?
> Everything under heaven belongs to me.
> (41:11)

These words of God are an echo of Job's acknowledgement in his wisdom poem that God

> views the ends of the earth
> and sees everything under the heavens.
> (28:24)

In chapter 41(as in chapter 28) the fear of God is powerfully underlined. "The thrust of this passage is: 'Fear him ye saints, and you will have nothing else to fear.'"[21]

Application: Can God be Trusted?

It will be helpful to put God's words to Job into the modern context. Job, in essence, has been challenging God with the question, "Why do you allow so much evil in the world?" This is a question that has been asked by many who have been deeply impacted by the Holocaust and other horrific events of recent history. In his historical and biographical novel *Night* Elie Wiesel describes his experience as a boy in the Nazi death camps. He recalls one

18. Reitman, *Unlocking Wisdom*, 160.
19. Ibid., 162–64.
20. Fyall, *Now My Eyes Have Seen You*, 174.
21. Ibid., 162.

incident in which a Jewish child was hung for a petty infraction. Because the child's weight was insufficient to snap his neck he dangled in mid-air, half alive and half-dead for several hours.[22] Why did God allow that? Some who have reflected on the "problem of evil" have concluded that either God is not all-loving and therefore does not have the desire to stop such gratuitous evil; or he is not all-powerful and therefore is unable to stop it. But God, in effect, turns the tables on questioners like Job and says, "I *am* your only hope!"

First there really cannot be such a thing as wickedness if there is not a living, holy, and just God who created the moral order in the first place and judges mankind according to it. To put it another way, without God there isn't a "problem of evil." For evil to exist there must be a real good; but in a totally naturalistic universe without God there is no objective standard of good, only personal preference. In his groundbreaking book, *From Darwin to Hitler*, intellectual historian Richard Weikart explains how Hitler was able to justify infanticide, eugenics, euthanasia, and racial genocide on the basis of the "survival of the fittest" principle of naturalistic evolution. Rejecting the Judeo-Christian proscription of killing innocent human life and spurning the idea of "natural rights" as a product of weaklings, Hitler exclaimed that "there is only one most holy right" and "holy duty," namely keep one's blood pure in order to "promote a more noble evolution" of humanity.[23] Hitler derided any morality inimical to the increased vitality of the Aryan race, particularly the Judeo-Christian principles of humility, pity, and sympathy. And he believed that the interests of the Aryan race as a "superior" race could best be promoted through encouraging the reproduction of the "highest individuals" within that race and getting rid of "inferior" individuals.[24] Of course, this naturalistic ethic necessarily led to a slippery slope of moral relativism and nihilism, for it depended on preconceived notions of "human improvement" which had no basis other than Hitler's own will to power. This also helps to explain why so many educated Germans could cooperate with the Nazis and participate in the Holocaust, as Hitler was drawing on ideas that were prevalent within German society at the time, particularly among the medical and scientific elites.[25]

The second inference from God's words to Job is that only he has the power to bring good out of evil and ultimately destroy evil itself. In his

---

22. Wiesel, *Night*, 64–65.
23. Weikart, *From Darwin to Hitler*, 214.
24. Ibid.
25. Ibid., 232.

The Lord Speaks

popular book *When Bad Things Happen to Good People* Harold Kushner affirms the goodness of God—that he is the source of charity, justice, and human dignity. But he denies that God is all-powerful. Forced to choose between a God who is good and a God who is not all-powerful, Kushner argues, the author of the book of Job chooses to believe in God's goodness. Thus when he describes the power of the sea serpent Leviathan (41:12–34), God is saying in effect that even he has difficulty keeping chaos in check and preventing evil from claiming innocent victims.[26] But, as we have seen, the whole point of God's speeches is to emphasize his power. Yancey effectively argues, "The final climactic scene offered God a perfect platform from which to discuss his lack of power, if indeed that was the problem." But God doesn't do that. Instead, Job 38–41 "contains as impressive a description of God's power as you will find anywhere in the Bible."[27] Admittedly, Job does not stress the final smiting and destruction of Leviathan. But this is implied in God's providence and control over the whole created universe. It is also the whole point of the final scene where, after Job repents in dust and ashes, God fully restores his health and prosperity. Job's blessing prefigures the eventual restoration of God's dominion over all of creation.[28] As Yancey further states:

> The Bible stakes God's reputation on his ability to conquer evil and restore heaven and earth to their original perfection. Apart from that future . . . God could be judged less-than-powerful or less-than-loving . . . Evil, not good, appears to be winning. But the Bible calls us to see beyond the grim reality of history to the view of all eternity, when God's reign will fill the earth with light and truth.[29]

---

26. Kushner, *When Bad Things Happen to Good People*, 42–43.
27. Yancey, *Where is God When It Hurts?*, 107.
28. Reitman, *Unlocking Wisdom*, 170.
29. Yancey, *Disappointment with God*, 243–44.

Conclusion

Toward a Practical Theology of Suffering

It is telling that the Bible does not contain a theological treatise on suffering. Rather, it tells us the story of one man's experience. This raises the question: Why does the book of Job take the form of a story? In this final chapter I will suggest that the story format is foundational for developing a practical theology of suffering. In particular, the use of story is important in three respects. First, it integrates theodicy with a pastoral understanding of suffering. Secondly, there is the power of understanding one's "life story" in that it helps one to reflect, discern, and discover more of God's unique handiwork in his or her life. In part, we see our story in Job's story. And, third, there is the connection between Job's story (and, by implication, the believer's personal story) and the larger story of God's redemptive purpose through the cross.

A Holistic and Integrated Approach to Suffering

In this study I have suggested that the book of Job integrates theodicy with a pastoral approach to suffering. The two approaches are not mutually exclusive. Sometimes when persons who suffer ask questions like "Why did this happen?" or "Where is God?" they are expressing sorrow and complaint in need of comfort. At other times they may be expressing an existential problem about whether to continue to believe in God, which requires a theoretical or theological answer that brings faith and hope. What is needed is practical wisdom to discern what is asked for and what is needed. What

Toward a Practical Theology of Suffering

is appropriate in one context may be inappropriate and even harmful in another. There are good ways and bad ways to communicate biblical truths and propositions.[1]

Ultimately, theodicy involves a search for truths about God. As such, it raises deep spiritual issues and invites a more engaged spirituality. But the experience of pain is not always adequately addressed by first giving spiritual and theological reasons or responses to suffering. The most appropriate immediate response to a person who is in extreme hunger and suffering from a serious illness, for example, may be to give food and medical care not offer ultimate explanations for why there is poverty, disease, and hunger in the world. This invites us to consider the linkage of spirit and body.[2] The importance of this linkage is indicated by clinical studies of pain:

> One very important insight is that physical pain is like a key that naturally unlocks caged spiritual issues. In turn, spiritual issues take over, redefine, compound, and intensify the person's response to physical pain. Researchers in the area of patient care and pain management find that pain is most effectively managed when a holistic approach to care of persons (as opposed to treatment of patients or, even worse, management of diseases) is modeled.[3]

If persons are spiritual, physical, and emotional/psychological beings, then an adequate response to suffering requires an approach that seeks total healing of the suffering person—or what has been termed *integrative wellness*.[4] As Natalie Weaver points out, all persons deal with issues of relationship, forgiveness, and meaning. Sometimes these issues which require close attention in periods of pain and suffering will overshadow more strictly theological or spiritual approaches. At other times, suffering may open up the opportunities to restore or enter into a new, more authentic relationship with God. Or, it may force caregivers themselves to re-examine the adequacy of their own beliefs and religious assumptions. As we have seen, the particular approach used by Job's three friends, though well intentioned, is ill-timed and involved a serious misapplication of spiritual principles to Job's particular situation. At the same time, Job's lament, while necessary to his ultimate healing, also involves some serious misconceptions about God's intentions and character. God uses suffering in Job's life to reveal

---

1 See Sovik "Why Almost all Moral Critique of Theodicies is Misplaced," 479–84.
2. Weaver, *Theology of Suffering and Death*, 12.
3. Ibid., 13.
4. Ibid.

deeper truths about himself and his involvement in Job's life. "In short, the manner in which we suffer and also care for the suffering of others reveals a great deal about who we are and how adequate our religious belief systems are for support on the journey."[5]

Determining the Shape of Your Story

Following the terrorist attacks of 9/11 the news media was filled with stories of those who lost their lives and of family members whose own lives were forever changed by this national tragedy. For a brief period we became a nation of stories.[6] These stories made it more possible for us to go beyond mere statistics (as horrific as this event was) and feel someone else's pain. Similarly, we cannot fully enter into the painful experiences of our own life unless we know our story.[7] In his insightful book *To Be Told*, Dan Allender discusses the importance of telling one's story. He writes:

> Everyone has a story. Put another way, everyone's life *is* a story. But most people don't know how to read their life in a way that reveals their story. They miss the deeper meaning in their life, and they have little sense of how God has written their story to reveal himself and his own story.[8]

However, the fact is that our lives are not a series of random events. God is not merely the Creator of our life. He is also the Author who writes the story of our lives to make something known about himself. Furthermore, he invites us to participate as a co-author in the writing of that story.[9] But it is only as we come to understand our particular story and our own part in composing it that we can discover its deepest meaning and what God has designed for us to reveal through it.[10]

Tragedy is an inevitable part of living under the curse of the Fall. We are part of the brokenness of creation. But, as Allender reminds us, tragedy and suffering also awaken our passions in ways that times of calm, blessing, and joy cannot. In fact, the word *passion* derives from a Latin root that means

---

5. Ibid.
6. Allender, *To Be Told*, 110.
7. Ibid.
8. Ibid., 1.
9. Ibid., 3.
10. Ibid., 6.

Toward a Practical Theology of Suffering

"suffering." "All passion is founded on pain, grown through risk, and marked by decisions we make in the face of tragedy."[11] Tragic events and suffering reveal the deepest things about ourselves—our passions and what we say either "yes" or "no" to. Pivotal tragedies also play a critical role in shaping our identity. They "set in motion the plot of a person's life."[12] As Job's story illustrates, times of suffering and tragedy can reveal the hand of God. They help fulfill our calling to make known something about God and his purposes that is bound up with our own unique character, experience, and story.[13] In fact, part of the universal appeal of the book of Job is that, to some extent at least, we can see our story reflected in Job's story. Knowing his story helps us better understand our own particular story and God's part in writing it. Like Job, we can move from brokenness to redemption and a revealing of divine glory. In an even larger sense, then, tragedy can be used to connect our story with the larger story of God's redemptive grace. God reinterprets our story in light of his story, or the grand narrative of redemption.

Job in the Larger Theological Context of the Cross

Some commentators have suggested that Job is in some respects a foreshadowing of Christ.[14] This is indicated by the various parallels as well as differences that we see between Job's story and the life of Christ. Both are tempted by Satan. As the Accuser, the devil tempts Job to curse and reject God. Through his trials Job maintains his belief in God, though he does at times question God's goodness. Jesus, on the other hand, is tempted by the devil to misuse his power and authority, though without sinning. Both Job and Jesus are innocent sufferers. Like Job, who feels abandoned by God, Jesus calls out on the cross, "God, why have you forsaken me?" Nonethe-

---

11. Ibid., 73–74.
12. Ibid., 75.
13. Ibid., 102.
14. Greg Parsons rightly cautions that we must avoid reading the New Testament back into the Old Testament. The book of Job must be understood on its own terms and within its own historical context. However, this does not negate the conclusion made by various writers that without the New Testament the Old Testament is incomplete and that the ultimate fulfillment of Job's message is found in Jesus Christ. Parsons argues that we must "balance the Old Testament context with input from the New Testament." ("Guidelines," 410) For example, in his commentary on Job, Norman Habel suggests that in preparation for Easter Sunday the expositor preach a series of sermons in which he views Job's major struggles in the context of Jesus' passion. (*Book of Job*, 10–12.)

less, both are faithful. But there are also crucial differences. Job is relatively innocent while Christ is the only truly innocent sufferer.[15] Job experiences God's grace *in* his suffering and is *rescued from* his afflictions. By contrast, Christ is the "Suffering Servant" (Isa. 53) who mediates God's grace and redeems mankind *through his suffering* and death on the cross; and is victorious over Satan and evil *through* his death and resurrection.[16]

This picture of Job as in some sense a prefiguring of Christ and the cross is significant in three ways for constructing a more complete theology of suffering. First, the cross points to the fact that God is not immune or detached from the suffering of the world. Traditionally, theologians have held to the view of the "impassability of God," or the belief that because he is perfect God cannot suffer. However, I agree with D. A. Carson who argues that the God who is left seems too much like Buddha, not the Father who saw his Son hang on the cross. "Here, then, the cross is climactic. God's plan of redemption cost the Father his Son; it cost the Son his life. And the Son learned suffering in *human terms* (Heb 2:14–15)."[17] Moreover, if we say that the sufferings of Christ are restricted to his human nature, are we not in danger of constructing an almost schizophrenic Christ?[18] Yancey rightly states that suffering was the cost to God of forgiveness. "Human suffering remains meaningless and barren unless we have some assurance that God is sympathetic to our pain, and can somehow heal that pain. In Jesus, we have that assurance."[19]

Secondly, taking up the cross means that we follow the example of Christ. The apostle Peter calls Christians to this "shared suffering" when he states:

> But if you suffer for doing good and you endure it, this is commendable before God. To this you were called, because Christ suffered for you, leaving you an example that you should follow in his steps. (1 Pet 2:20–21)

---

15. Keller, *Walking With God through Pain and Suffering*, 292–93.

16. John Hartley draws numerous parallels between Job and the "Suffering Servant" songs of Isaiah, but adds that the idea of "vicarious suffering" is merely hinted at in Job. He suggests therefore that "the message of Job prepared the people to understand and receive Isaiah's bold new message that God was going to redeem his people through the innocent suffering of his obedient servant." (*Book of Job*, 14–15)

17. Carson, *How Long, O Lord?*, 167.

18. Ibid., 165.

19. Yancey, *Where is God When It Hurts?*, 160.

Toward a Practical Theology of Suffering

Just as Christ suffered unjustly, those who follow him can also expect to suffer unfairly. The apostle Paul describes this experience of identification with Christ in suffering in terms of being united with him (Phil 2:1). But this very experience also enables us to better identify with and serve others who suffer, including those who are also innocent victims of injustice. This "cruciform love" seeks mercy and justice for "crucified people."[20] Henri Nouwen causes us to reflect deeply on the meaning of sharing in Christ's sufferings when he asks, "Who can take away suffering without entering it?"[21] He continues:

> It is an illusion to think that a person can be led out the desert by someone who has never been there. Our lives are filled with examples telling us that leadership requires understanding, and understanding requires sharing, So long as we define leadership . . . in terms of being responsible for some kind of abstract "general good," we have forgotten that no God can save us except a suffering God, and that no one can lead others except the one who is crushed by their sins.[22]

Compassion, which means "to suffer with," involves both a participation in the brokenness of the world and the effort to speak prophetically from the perspective of the woundedness which we all share.[23] This concept of "suffering with" recognizes the critical importance of prayer (or what Nouwen calls "sensitive articulation"[24]) for the healing of the inner spirit. In Job, the prayer before God in the form of lament is basically a cry for help, for himself and others. This dual articulation of one's own suffering and that of others also guards against a form of religious piety that pretends to care for others but is actually preoccupied with mere religion.[25]

It is of course true, as the great evangelical theologian Jonathan Edwards argued, that a pastoral theology which is not grounded "first and last" in love for God is fundamentally flawed. This is the primary lesson

---

20. See Gorman, *Cruciformity*, 393.
21. Nouwen, *Wounded Healer*, 78.
22. Ibid.
23. Zylla, *Virtue as Consent to Being*, 120.
24. Ibid., 80, 114; Nouwen, *Wounded Healer*, 42.
25. Zylla, *Virtue as Consent to Being*, 112. I am speaking of "religion" here as mere intellectual adherence to certain doctrinal beliefs divorced from an active faith, which James describes in terms of moral purity and a protection of widows and orphans (Jas 1: 27; 2:14–19) and Paul characterizes as "faith expressing itself through love" (Gal 5:6).

of Job. However, such love is not disconnected from concern for the well-being of others, or what Edwards describes as seeking the "good of every individual being."[26] As Zylla argues, love for God and love for neighbor are not separate moral functions but part of an entire dynamic relational vision of the moral life.[27] In other words, a practical theology of suffering must flow from the interconnectedness of love for God and love for neighbor. Otherwise, we are left with theological and moral abstractions where "the words are correct, but they have no weight."[28]

Finally, the victory of the cross signifies hope for a new humanity and the restoration of the entire created order. I have argued throughout this study that Job's struggles with suffering are bound up with the travail at the heart of creation itself. This links Job's experience with Paul's description in Romans 8 of the threefold groaning, involving: 1) *creation*, which longs for eschatological renewal (vv. 20–22); 2) the *children of God* (or Christian community), who eagerly await their adoption as sons and the redemption of their bodies (v. 23); and 3) the *Spirit of God* who intercedes for us with groans "that words cannot express" (vv. 26–27). The Spirit who intercedes for us in our present suffering is the same Spirit who raised Jesus from the dead (v. 11) and guarantees future glory with him (v. 17).[29] So, while suffering often remains a mystery and will not end until there is the ultimate completion of God's redemptive purposes, we can also be confident that our present struggles are not without meaning or purpose.

When I was an undergraduate in college, my apologetics professor gave us an assignment which involved writing an essay in response to this question (or something like it): "What for you would be proof that there is not a loving God? Give reasons for your answer." This might seem like an odd assignment to give students in a Christian college! But it forced me to re-examine my Christian beliefs and assumptions about God. I do not remember the details of what I wrote. But, as I recall, my conclusion was

---

26. Ibid., 63. Edwards argues that, while love for God as the "Being of beings" is primary, the good or happiness of the creature is not to be thought of as separate from or independent of God's glory or happiness. The two are inseparable. For, in seeking his own glory God seeks the glory and happiness of the creature as well. Thus, true virtue will seek the good of every individual being insofar as it is consistent with seeking the highest good or love of God. See also Holbrook, *Ethics of Jonathan Edwards*, 109–10.

27. Zylla, *Virtue as Consent to Being*, 71.

28. This expression comes from Dietrich Bonhoeffer. See Zylla, *Virtue as Consent to Being*, 110.

29. Zylla, *The Roots of Sorrow*, 136–42.

that I could not believe in a loving and merciful God if there was proof that Christ did not die and rise from the dead. Back then, I did not fully understand the implications of my conclusion. But I am convinced that it is in the theology of the cross that one finds the most complete response to the problem of evil and the suffering of spirit, soul, and body in the world. The story of Job is part of the biblical witness that points us in this direction.

Appendix

Discussion Guide

While the book of Job can be studied alone, the topic of suffering is best addressed through group discussion where individuals can collectively share their insights and experiences as well as provide mutual support and encouragement. The optimum size for the group is eight to twelve participants, through a smaller group is certainly workable. Ideally, it should not exceed twelve people. Anything larger will tend to stifle group interaction and the study will probably revert to a "teacher–student" format.

Organization of the Study

I have arranged the chapters in the book so that the study itself can be covered in ten weeks (plus an introductory session and conclusion), though you may choose to make it longer.[1] I would suggest the following sequence:

1. Distribute materials to the participants one or two weeks prior to the beginning of the study with instructions to read the entire book of Job and the introduction to this book. Participants should also reflect on the questions for the introduction.

2. Introductory session: a) clarify the purpose of the study and discuss group guidelines; b) discuss group expectations—that is, what do participants hope to gain from the study?; c) go over discussion questions

---

[1]. Note: Chapters 1–10 in the book correspond to weeks 1–10 in this discussion guide.

for the introduction; and d) answer any further questions that people might have.

3. Weeks 1–10: formal study of Job. Below are the chapters in the book of Job that should be read in conjunction with each week's study:
   a. Week 1: (1:1–19; 29:1–30:31; 42:1–6)
   b. Weeks 2–4 (1:1–2:10)
   c. Week 5 (3:1–26; 42:1–16
   d. Week 6 (2:11–13; 4:1–5; 27)
   e. Week 7 (16:1–17:16; 24:1–25)
   f. Week 8 (26:1–31:40)
   g. Week 9 (32:1–37:24)
   h. Week 10 (38:1–42:1–6)

4. Conclusion: discuss the questions and make a final summary.

Leading the Discussion

The study will be most effective if there is a designated leader. If you are the leader, a willingness to open up and share life experiences will help others in the group do the same. Do not worry if you are unable to cover all of the questions. If there is interest in a particular topic, you may choose to extend the discussion one more week. On the other hand, don't feel bound by this book's structure. If you get bogged down on a particular topic that is of less interest to the group move on to a something that is more conducive to group interaction. Follow your instincts based on your sense of the particular needs and concerns of group members. This study is intended to be practical, so make sure that you also leave enough time for personal and group application. Group discussion works best when people have read the relevant materials beforehand. So, strongly encourage the participants to read the chapter in the book and relevant chapters in the book of Job *before* the discussion. Here are some further guidelines for leading the group discussion:

1. Facilitate discussion as much as possible, without lecturing.
2. Don't allow one person to monopolize the discussion.
3. Be positive and affirming of people as much as possible. Be supportive with comments like: "I've felt that way too," or "I understand where you're coming from."

Discussion Guide

4. Stay on the topic as much as possible and avoid rabbit trails. If you feel that the discussion is getting off track try to get back on course by saying, "Could we go back to something that was said earlier?"
5. Set firm guidelines for sharing and confidentiality.
6. Promote further discussion on a given comment by raising further questions ("When did you begin to feel that way?"); or by asking for clarification ("Do you mean to say ... or do you mean ... ?")
7. Don't worry if you're asked a question you can't answer. Say, "I honestly don't know; but I will try to find out."
8. Begin and end with prayer.

Introduction

Read the entire book of Job in several sittings. A possible schedule would be as follows:
    a. First sitting: chaps. 1–14
    b. Second sitting: chaps. 15–31
    c. Third sitting: chaps. 32–42

1. After reading the entire book, what do you think is its main message? Complete this sentence: "The main purpose of the book of Job is ... "
2. Note the following literary genres:
    a. Epic narrative (1:1–2:13)
    b. Lament (3:1–26)
    c. Praise hymn (9:5–13)
    d. Proverb (6:14, 25a)
    e. Extended metaphor (6:15–19)
    f. Interrogation (38:4–39:30)
3. How does each of these genres contribute to the overall purpose of this book?
4. Of the three perspectives on Job discussed in the introduction, which do you identify with the most? Which do you think is least helpful in understanding this book?

DISCUSSION GUIDE

Week One: The Mission of God in the Book of Job

How does the author describe the "mission of God?" How is this concept related to the story of God's covenant with Israel in the Old Testament?

1. What are some allusions to God's covenant with Israel in the story of Job? Why is this important to understanding its overall message?
2. How is the Accuser's taunt "Does Job fear God for nothing?" (1:9a) the key to understanding the book of Job? Why is it important for us, especially in times of difficulty?
3. Discuss the following statement by Kayla Mueller: "Some people find God in Church, some people find God in nature, some people find God in love, I find God in suffering." Which of these ways of "finding God" is most descriptive of you?
4. Compare Kayla's statement "I find God in suffering" with the statement by a character in M.T. Anderson's Book, *The Astonishing Life of Octavian Nothing* that, "Kindness without the promise of profit is an impossibility." Which of these statements do you think is most applicable to the church today?
5. How can God be "revealed" in suffering? How is this "good news?"
6. How is the story of Job reflective of God redemptive mission in the world?
7. How does the story of Job shape and equip us for participation in God's mission in the world?
8. How can we "contextualize" the message of Job today?

Week Two: God's Ongoing Activity in His Creation

What is the significance of the biblical teaching that God is the Creator and Sustainer of the entire universe? What does this mean to you personally? What are some ways in which we can either affirm or deny this truth in our lives?

1. What is the importance as well as limits of the principle of "retribution?"

2. What is the significance for human relationships of the principle that we all share a common Maker? (See Job 31:13–15; cf. 22:5–11; 34:19, 28).

3. Read chapters 1 and 2 of Job. What descriptions or "word pictures" of God, the Accuser, and Job are given in these chapters?

4. What is the Accuser's main accusation against God (1: 9–11; cf. 2:4–5)?

5. In his commentary on Job, John Walton states that Christians in America tend to be motivated by an attitude of "what's in it for me?" Do you agree?

6. Why do you think the "prosperity gospel" is so popular in America today? What are some of the dangers of this perspective?

7. What do you think is the meaning of "disinterested faith/righteousness?" How can we apply this concept in our lives as Christians, especially during times of trial or suffering?

8. What else have you learned from this week's study that you can apply to your life?

Week Three: The Ambiguity and Unpredictability of Life

Two "big" questions that are often asked are: a) "Why do good people suffer?" and b) "Why do the wicked prosper?" Are there any examples of these from your own experience? What do you think are some possible answers to these questions?

1. The author states that we are uncomfortable with suffering—both with the prospect of it happening to us and when it happens to others. Do you agree? If so, why do you think this is the case?

2. Psychologists often distinguish between the "primary" (immediate) losses and the secondary losses (or additional losses "triggered" by the primary loss). What were Job's primary and secondary losses? Have you had similar experiences?

3. Consider the following responses that often accompany deep anger and disappointment in suffering and loss.[2] Have you ever had similar thoughts or reactions?

2. See Marr, *The Reluctant Traveler*, 51.

Discussion Guide

   a. I will never be the same
   b. It's not fair!
   c. I don't deserve this!
   d. People will always look at me differently now.
   e. Life is not worth living.
   f. This seems absolutely senseless.

4. What is the significance of the fact that Job is not privy to the "wager" between God and the Accuser?

5. What is the significance of the teaching in Scripture that we are acted upon by "unseen" spiritual forces (Eph 2:2; 1 Pet 5:8)?

6. Throughout this book God is depicted as "causing" Job's suffering. Why do you think God might "cause" or "allow" suffering to come into our lives? Do you think God is always the "cause" of suffering? Why or why not?

7. What is the significance of the difference between the "God concept" and "God image" for understanding Job?

8. Have you ever been in a situation where suffering has dramatically affected your or someone else's view of God and/or relationship to others (either positively or negatively)? If so, what was the eventual outcome of that experience?

9. What else have you learned from this chapter that you can apply to your life?

Week Four: The Fear of the Lord in Response to His Sovereignty

The author of this study states that "the fear of the Lord" is not popular in contemporary Christian culture. Do you agree? If so, why do you think this is the case?

1. How would you respond to someone who argues that tragedies are simply the result of blind physical chance?

2. Read Job 1:1–5; 8 and 2:3. How is Job described as "fearing the Lord" in these verses? What is the significance of this concept for understanding the book of Job?

Discussion Guide

3. Read Proverbs 1:7; 3:5–7; 8:13; 9:10; and Ecclesiastes 12:13–14. What is the meaning of the "fear of the Lord" in these verses?

4. Why is the "fear of the Lord" important for the Christian life?

5. How do Job and Ecclesiastes help us understand the importance of the fear of the Lord in responding to suffering?

6. In *Walking with God through Pain and Suffering* Timothy Keller quotes sociologist Peter Berger's observation that every culture has provided an "explanation of human events that bestow meaning upon the experiences of suffering and evil" (p. 14). What are some common responses to suffering in our contemporary culture? Can you give some examples?

7. Discuss G.K. Chesterton's portrayal of Job's suffering in *The Man Who Was Thursday*. What different worldviews or philosophies of suffering are represented by the main characters in this novel? Are there times when we might express one or more of these philosophies? Do you agree or disagree with Chesterton's explanation for why Job (and all Christians) have to suffer? Why or why not?

8. What else have you learned from this week's study that you can apply to your life?

Week Five: The Redemptive Grace of God

The author talks about Christian "triumphalism" and "escapism" in the church today. Can you give some examples? What does he say is the corrective to these two tendencies? Do you agree?

1. Compare what Job says in 1:20–22 and 2:10 with his lament in 3:3–26. How could such seemingly contradictory statements come from one person? What might explain the dramatic change in Job's attitude towards his suffering?

2. What is Job's "theology of creation" in 3:4–10 (cf. Ps 8:3; 147:4; 148:3)?

3. Compare what Job says in 3:23–24 with 13:15 and 19:25–26. What does this reveal about Job's experience in suffering? Are there times when you (or someone you know) have gone through similar experiences?

4. How are Job's words similar to what Paul says in Romans 8:18–21?

5. What does Job's experience reveal about the "revelation" and "hiddenness" of God? Why is this concept important for understanding suffering?

6. At the end of the story Job's possessions and health are restored and he is given more children (42:12–15). Why is this significant? How would you respond that this sneaks the "prosperity gospel" in through the "back door?"

7. Discuss Joni Eareckson Tada's description of her personal experience of suffering. How was she able to move from despair to hope, and even joy?

8. What else have you learned from this week's lesson that you can apply to your life?

Week Six: Job's Friends—The Moralistic Response to Suffering

The nature and quality of a person's "social support system" (i.e., family, friends, church) can make a big difference in one's ability to respond positively to suffering. Reflecting on your or someone else's experience of suffering or loss, how was it viewed by others? Was it responded to positively or negatively? Did it increase or decrease your (or his/her) status?

1. Read Job 2:11–13. In what ways did Job's friends initially respond positively to Job's suffering?

2. Eliphaz (one of Job's three friends) is the first to respond verbally to Job's suffering in 4:1–5:27. Read these verses. What is the substance of his explanation for Job's suffering? (See especially 4:1–9.) Do we often have a tendency to respond in the same manner to someone else's suffering or misfortune? Can you give some examples?

3. When we suffer or experience significant loss we may resort to bargaining with God. Marr describes this as "the hope that escape is possible, that by some fortunate twist of circumstances we will be granted power over our situation, and thus have the opportunity to shape the outcome to fit our needs."[3] How is the "advice" of Eliphaz in 5:8–27 and that of Bildad in 8:5–7 an example of "bargaining?"

---

3. Barr, *The Reluctant Traveler*, 70–71.

4. Have you ever made in bargains with God in response to suffering or major loss? What was the outcome? What impact did it have on your spiritual life?

5. What assumptions do we often make in a "moralistic" response to suffering? What is the element of truth in this type of response? What are some pitfalls?

6. What are some other "spiritual" answers that might be given to suffering? Zyla argues that (even if well intentioned and biblical) such responses can lead us to become "detached observers" who minimize suffering and fail to fully empathize with the sufferer.[4] Do you agree? If so, how can this be avoided?

7. What else have you learned from this week's lesson that you can apply to your life?

Week Seven: Job's Lament—Honesty Before God

Why do you think the importance of biblical lament is often downplayed in Christian culture?

1. Silence often precedes verbal lament (Job 3:13; cf. Rom 8:26). Why do you think this is the case?

2. Read Job 16:1–17:16. Here Job identifies and names his pain. Diane Marr states, "The initial step in any healing process is to recognize the need for healing. Regardless of the type or magnitude of our loss, we must first be willing and able to identify our loss as *loss*."[5] Why is "naming" or "identifying" your pain important? What are some ways in which people might ignore, deny, or devalue their loss or pain? Why do people avoid naming their loss?

3. What types or dimensions of pain and suffering does Job express in chapters 16 and 17? Are you able to "vent" painful feelings and experiences in these areas?

4. Why is a multidimensional and holistic response to suffering important?

---

4. Zyla, *Roots of Sorrow*, 12–13, 23–30.
5. Barr, *The Reluctant Traveler*, 21.

5. Read Job 24:1–25. How does Job describe the injustices that are committed against the poor, fatherless, and the needy? Why do you think Job raises the issue of social justice in the context of his own suffering? Why is this important?

6. Compare what Job says in 24:1 with Jer. 12:1–2 and Hab. 1:1–4, 13. Have you ever wondered why the wicked prosper and good people suffer injustice? What are some examples of this in our day? Biblically, what should be the Christian response to this state of affairs?

7. Mental health experts remind us that healing from catastrophic loss or deep trauma is a process, not an event. Are there times when you (like Job) have alternated between hope and despair? What are some things that can exacerbate this cycle? Have you ever had people tell you to "get on with your life" before you were ready?

8. Spiritually, how can a person who has experienced loss and/or trauma move from lament to praise?

9. What else have you learned from this week's study that you can apply to your life?

Week Eight: Where is Wisdom to be Found?

Read chapter 26. How does Job describe God? How can Job's understanding of God in this chapter be reconciled with what he says in 27: 2?

1. The author states that Job's "oath of imprecation" in 27:7–10 is actually important to his ultimate healing. Do you agree? Why or why not?

2. Job's speeches in chapters 26 and 27 mark the end of his "dialogue" with his friends. What is the significance of this?

3. Read chapter 28. How does Job describe true wisdom? How does this contrast with "worldly" wisdom?

4. Despite the many truths contained in the poem to wisdom in chapter 28, why does it fall short of providing the ultimate solution to Job's dilemma? What does he have yet to discover? How is this instructive for us?

5. How does Job describe his righteousness in 29:11–17 and 31:1–34?

6. In 30:26 Job cries out, "Yet when I hoped for good, evil came; when I looked for light, then came darkness." What is Job saying? (Consider the larger context of this verse.) What is the error in this type of thinking? Have you ever felt like Job that life is fundamentally unfair? What did God teach you in that experience?

7. Despite Job's many protestations, God ultimately vindicates Job while he rebukes his friends who are commanded to offer burnt offerings. Job is even told to offer a prayer for his friends! (42:7–9). Why do you think God responds in this way? What does Job do that his friends fail to do?

8. Have you ever had the same questions and doubts about God's goodness as are expressed by Job as well as by C.S. Lewis in *A Grief Observed*? If so, how did you work through those feelings? What can we learn from Lewis' and Job's experience?

9. In the last chapter of *A Grief Observed* Lewis states:

> Grief is like a long valley, a long winding valley where any new bend may reveal a totally new landscape. Sometimes the surprise is the opposite one; you are presented with exactly the same sort of country you thought you had left behind miles ago. That is when you wonder whether the valley isn't a circular trench. But it isn't. There are partial recurrences, but the sequence doesn't repeat."[6]

What is Lewis getting at? How is this picture reflective of Job's experience? Is it helpful to describe suffering and grief in this way? Why or why not?

Week Nine: Elihu's Theology—Suffering as an Instrument of God's Redemptive Purpose

God does not rebuke Elihu as he does Job's friends nor does God praise him. Why do you think this is the case? What do you think he gets right; and what does he get wrong? Does he say things which are correct but express them poorly?

1. John Swinton describes "practical theodicy" as addressing the question, "How can people continue to love God in the midst of suffering

---

6. Lewis, *A Grief Observed*, 60.

and pain?" How is Elihu's response to Job an example of this type of theodicy?

2. Elihu takes issue with Job's complaint about God's silence by stating: "For God does speak—now one way, now another—though man may not perceive it" (33:14). What are some of the ways that God may be speaking, according to Elihu? Read:
    a. 33:19–30
    b. 34:14, 33
    c. 36:15–16

3. In 36:21 Elihu warns Job, "Beware of turning to evil, which you seem to prefer to affliction." Put this verse into your own words.

4. Timothy Keller observes that a "toxic effect" of affliction is that it can involve the temptation of *complicity* or unhealthy acceptance. This can take the form of self-pity which becomes "sweet and addicting." Or affliction can "become a great excuse for all sorts of behavior or pattern of life you could not otherwise justify."[7] Can you give some examples of what Keller (and Elihu) are cautioning against? When we suffer or experience pain, how can we avoid these temptations?

5. Read 35:9–16. What is Elihu warning against? Compare what Elihu says here with Psalm 34:15–16; 66:18 and James 1:6–8. Do you think Job's prayers are impeded by his attitude? When we suffer or experience pain or deep disappointment, how might our attitude affect God's response to us?

6. In his laments Job is very honest in expressing his feelings before God. He expresses his complaints, doubts, anger, and pain directly to God. When does such honesty become sinful?

7. What are some dangers of a theology of "virtuous suffering?" How can these dangers be avoided?

Week Ten: The Lord Speaks—Finding Meaning, Security, and Hope in God

Job 38:1 states, "Then the Lord answered Job out of the storm." What features of this response indicate that God has not come to crush or judge Job but to reach out in grace? Why is this important?

---

7. Keller, *Walking with God in Pain and Suffering*, 215.

Discussion Guide

1. Throughout chapters 38 and 39 God responds to Job with a series of questions (i.e., "Where were you when I laid the earth's foundations? . . . " "Have you ever given orders to the morning? . . . " "Do you know the laws of the heavens? . . . " etc.) What is the significance of these questions to Job? What do they reveal about the misconceptions that Job has about God?

2. In his book *Your God is Too Small*, J. B. Phillips argues that even as Christians we often have inadequate conceptions of God which linger unconsciously in our minds and which prevent us from catching a glimpse of the true God.[8] What are some inadequate conceptions of God that we might have, particularly in times of loss, trauma, and suffering? How does God's response to Job correct these deficient views?

3. The author argues that an appropriate response to suffering involves an integration of the psychological and spiritual in three areas: 1) achieving a sense of security; 2) discovering meaning and purpose; and 3) finding hope in suffering. How does God's response to Job in chapters 38–39 meet his needs in these three areas?

4. What can we learn from Anthony Flew's "vacation scenario?"

5. Job's initial response to God's first speech is given in 40:4–5. What can we learn from this response?

6. What do you think is the meaning of God's words to Job in 40:8–10? How do these words apply to those who would presume to question God's justice?

7. What do chapters 40 and 41 reveal about God's moral governance of the universe?

8. Discuss Job's response to God's second speech (40:1–6). What can we learn from Job's final response?

Conclusion: Toward a Practical Theology of Suffering

Why do you think the book of Job takes the form of a story?

1. What is "integrated wellness?" Why is this important in addressing suffering?

---

8. Phillips, *Your God is Too Small*, 8.

Discussion Guide

2. Take a separate sheet of paper and turn it to "landscape." Then, draw a straight horizontal line lengthwise across the middle. At the top, write "high points" and at the bottom write "hard times." Plot major events in your life by describing important high points above the line and hard times (trials, difficulties, major loss, suffering, etc.) below the line. If you feel creative, draw images that represent the high and low points in your life. Indicate the ages at which these events occurred. If you feel comfortable doing so, share your story line with the rest of the group.

3. What element(s) in the story of Job most resonate with you? How does it help you in understanding your own story?

4. How have major events in your life shaped who you are today? How have you seen God's character revealed in these events?

5. Dan Allender writes,

   > The future is meant to be written in light of the patterns of the past. We can't predict the future, but we can read the patterns of the past to see how God has marked us for his purposes. He uses the past to open our future. As we learn to read patterns, we gain an understanding of our calling."[9]

   How do the past events of your life help you discern God's purposes for you? Complete this sentence: "Based on the trajectory of my life, my purpose is . . . "

6. Do you agree with Nouwen that we can help those who suffer only if we ourselves have suffered? If so, how have the tragedies, difficulties, and trials in your life prepared you to help others who suffer?

7. Why is the cross of Christ of crucial importance in dealing with the suffering that comes into our lives and the lives of others whom we love?

8. What are some key lessons that you have learned from this study of the book of Job?

---

9. Allender, *To Be Told*, 92.

Bibliography

Allender, Dan B. *To Be Told: Know Your Story, Shape Your Future*. Colorado Springs: WaterBrook, 2005.

Andersen, Francis I. *Job: An Introduction and Commentary: Tyndale Old Testament Commentaries*. Downers Grove: IVP, 1976.

Anderson, Kim M. *Enhancing Resilience in Survivors of Family Violence*. New York: Springer, 2010.

Bartholomew, Craig G., and Ryan P. O'Dowd, *Old Testament Wisdom Literature: A Theological Introduction*. Downers Grove: IVP, 2011.

Bricker, Daniel P. "The Doctrine of the 'Two Ways' in Proverbs." *Journal of the Evangelical Theological Society* 38, no. 4 (December 1995) 501–17.

Brueggermann, Walter. "The Costly Loss of Lament." *Journal for the Study of the Old Testament*, 36 (1986) 57–71.

Bullock, C. Hassel. *An Introduction to Old Testament Poetic Books*. Chicago: Moody, 1988.

———. "Wisdom, the 'Amen' of Torah." *Journal of the Evangelical Theological Society* 52, no. 1 (March 2009) 6–18.

Cannon, Elsie. *Social Justice Handbook: Small Steps for a Better World*. Downers Grove: IVP, 2009

Capps, Kory. "Comfort In Strange Places: Musings on the Book of Job." https://korycapps.files.wordpress.com/2013/10/comfort-in-job-g-g-format.pdf.

Carson, D. A. *How Long, O Lord? Reflections on Suffering and Evil*. Grand Rapids: Baker, 1999, 2006

Castelo, Daniel. "The Fear of the Lord as Theological Method." *Journal of Theological Interpretation* 2 no. 1 (2008) 147–160.

Chesterton, G. K. *The Man Called Thursday: A Nightmare*. New York: Dodd, Mead & Co., 1908.

———. *Orthodoxy*. New York: John Lane, 1908.

Cook, Carol J., and Cindy L. Guertin, "How Childhood Sexual Abuse Affects Adult Survivors' Images of God: A Resource for Pastoral Helpers," *Sacred Spaces: The e-Journal of the American Association for Pastoral Counselors* 2 (2010) 38–55. http://www.aapc.org/_templates/74/cookguertin.pdf

Coutts, Jon Randall. "A Tale of Emptied Hells: The Apologetics of G.K. Chesterton in The Man Who Was Thursday." PhD diss., Asbury Seminary, 2008. http://place.asburyseminary.edu/trendissertations/8268

Bibliography

Davies, Paul. *The 5th Miracle: The Search for the Origin and Meaning of Life.* New York: Touchstone, 1999.

Davy, Timothy James. "The Book of Job and the Mission of God: An Application of a Missional Hermeneutic to the Book of Job." PhD diss., University of Gloucestershire, 2014. http://eprints.glos.ac.uk/id/eprint/2271

Dawkins, Richard. *The God Delusion.* New York: Houghton and Mifflin, 2006.

———. *River Out of Eden: A Darwinian View of Life.* New York: Basic Books, 1996.

Elliott, Neil. *Liberating Paul: The Justice of God and the Politics of the Apostle.* Maryknoll: Orbis, 1994.

Eppinette, Matthew. "Human 2.0: Transhumanism as a Cultural Trend." In *Everyday Theology: How to Read Cultural Texts and Interpret Trends*, edited by Kevin J. Vanhoozer, Charles A. Anderson, and Michael J. Sleasman, 191–207. Grand Rapids: Baker Academic, 2007.

Eswine, Zach. *Recovering Eden: The Gospel According to Ecclesiastes.* Phillipsburg: R&R, 2014

Fee, Gordon D., and Douglas Stuart, *How to Read the Bible for All Its Worth: A Guide to Understanding the Bible.* Grand Rapids: Zondervan, 1993.

Feinberg, John S. *Deceived By God? A journey Through Suffering.* Wheaton: Crossway, 1997.

Fernando, Ajith. *The Call to Joy and Pain: Embracing Suffering in Your Ministry.* Wheaton: Crossway, 2007).

Flew, Anthony. *There is a God: How the World's Most Notorious Atheist Changed His Mind.* New York: HarperOne, 2007.

Fyall, Robert S. *Now My Eyes Have Seen You: Images of Creation and Evil in the Book of Job.* Downers Grove: IVP, 2002.

Gerhardt, Elizabeth. *The Cross and Gendercide: A Theological Response to Global Violence Against Women and Girls.* Downers Grove: IVP Academic, 2014.

Goheen, Michael W. *Introducing Christian Mission Today: Scripture, History, and Issues.* Downers Grove: IVP Academic, 2014.

Goldingay, John. "The 'Salvation History' Perspective and the 'Wisdom' Perspective within the Context of Biblical Theology." *Evangelical Quarterly* 51 (1979) 194–207.

———. *Theological Diversity and the Authority of the Old Testament.* Grand Rapids, MI: Eerdmans, 1987.

Gorman, Michael J. *Cruciformity: Paul's Narrative Spirituality of the Cross.* Grand Rapids: Eerdmans, 2001.

Gutierrez, Gustavo. *On Job: God-Talk and the Suffering of the Innocent.* Maryknoll: Orbis, 1987.

Habel, Norman C. *The Book of Job: A Commentary.* Louisville: Westminster John Knox, 1985.

Hagin, Kenneth. "Faith for Prosperity." http://hopefaithprayer.com/faith/kenneth-hagin-faith-lesson-no-15-faith-for-prosperity/

Harris, Elise and Alan Holdren, "'I find God in suffering': The gripping life and death of Kayla Mueller." *Catholic News Agency* (May 1, 2015). http://www.catholicnewsagency.com/news/i-find-god-in-suffering-the-gripping-life-and-death-of-kayla-mueller-10924/

Hartley, John E. *The Book of Job.* Grand Rapids: Eerdmans, 1988.

Herman, Judith Lewis. *Trauma and Recovery.* New York: Basic Books, 1992.

Bibliography

Hesselgrave, Ronald P. *The JustMissional Church: Pursuing God's Path for Justice.* CreateSpace, 2014.

Hoffman, Louis, Christopher S.M. Grimes, and Michael C. Mitchell. "Transcendence, Suffering, and Psychotherapy." Paper originally presented at the 3rd International Conference on Personal Meaning, Vancouver, British Columbia, Canada, July 2004. https:// www.academia.edu/1707076/

Holbrook, Clyde A. *The Ethics of Jonathan Edwards: Morality and Aesthetics.* Ann Arbor: University of Michigan Press, 1973.

Hooks, Stephen. *College Press NIV Commentary: Job.* Joplin, MO: College Press, 2007.

Hubble, Rosemary A. *Conversation of the Dung Heap.* Collegeville, MN: Liturgical, 1998.

International Labor Office, *Profits and Poverty: The Economics of Forced Labor.* Geneva: IL: 2014.

Janzen, Gerald J. *At the Scent of Water: The Ground of Hope in the Book of Job.* Grand Rapids: Eerdmans, 2009.

Kaiser, Walter C. Jr. *Mission in the Old Testament: Israel as a Light to the Nations.* Grand Rapids: Baker, 2000.

———. "The Old Testament Promise of Material Blessings and the Contemporary Believer." *Trinity Journal* 9 (NS) 151–170.

———. "Wisdom Theology and the Centre of Old Testament Theology." *The Evangelical Quarterly* 50 (1978) 132–146.

Keller, Timothy. *Walking with God through Pain and Suffering.* New York: Dutton, 2013.

Kidner, Derek. *Tyndale Old Testament Commentaries: Proverbs.* Downers Grove, IL: IVP, 1975.

Kushner, Harold S. *The Book of Job: When Bad Things Happened to a Good Person.* New York: Schocken, 2012.

———. *When Bad Things Happen to Good People.* New York: Avon, 1981.

Lee, Young Hoon. "The Case for Prosperity Theology." *Evangelical Review of Theology* 20, no. 1 (1996) 26–39.

Lewis, C. S. *A Grief Observed.* New York: HarperCollins, 2001.

———. *The Problem of Pain.* New York: Macmillan, 1962

Linthicum, Robert. *Transforming Power: Biblical Strategies for Making a Difference in Your Community* Downers Grove: IVP, 2003.

Lo, Alison. *Job 28 As Rhetoric: An Analysis of Job 28 in the Context of Job 22-31, Volume 97* Leiden: Brill, 2003.

Louw, Daniel J. "Virtuous Suffering and the Predicament of Being Handicapped: Towards a Theology of the 'Disabled God Puffing in a Wheelchair,'" *In die Skriflig/In Luce Verbi* 48, no. 1 (2014) 1–10. http://www.indieskriflig.org.za/index.php/skriflig/article/view/ 1692, p. 5.

Luevano, Rafael. *Woman-Killing In Juarez: Theodicy at the Border.* New York: Orbis, 2012

Marr, Diane Dempsey. *The Reluctant Traveler: A Pilgrimage Through Loss and Recovery.* Colorado Springs: Navipress, 2002.

Marshall, Chris. "Divine Justice as Restorative." *Center for Christian Ethics* (2012) 11–19. http://www.baylor.edu/content/ services/document.php/ 163072.pdf

Mathewson, Dan. "Between Testimony and Interpretation: The Book of Job in Post-Holocaust, Jewish Theological Reflection." *Studies in the Literary Imagination* 41, no. 2 (2008): 17–39.

Middleton, J. Richard. "Why the 'Greater Good' Isn't a Defense: Classical Theodicy in Light of the Biblical Genre of Lament," *Koinonia* 9, nos. 1 & 2 (1997) 81–113.

Bibliography

Moriarty, Glen. *Pastoral Care of Depression: Helping Clients Heal Their Relationship with God*. New York: Routledge, 2012.

Nouwen, Henri J. M. *The Wounded Healer: Ministry in Contemporary Society*. New York: Doubleday, 1979).

Osteen, Joel. *Break Out! Five Keys to Go Beyond Your Barriers and Live an Extraordinary Life*. New York: Faith Words, 2013.

Osborne, Grant R. *The Hermeneutical Spiral: A Comprehensive Introduction to Biblical Interpretation*. Downers Gove: IVP, 1991.

Parsons, Greg W. "Guidelines for Understanding and Proclaiming the Book of Job." *Bibliotheca Sacra* 151 (October–December 1994) 393–413.

Phillips, Elaine A. "Speaking Truthfully: Job's Friends and Job," *Bulletin for Biblical Research* 18, no.1 (2008) 31–43.

Piper, John. *Don't Waste Your Life*. Wheaton: Crossway, 2007.

Pleins, David J. *The Social Visions of the Hebrew Bible: A Theological Introduction*. Louisville: Westminster John Knox, 2001.

Postell, Allison."Wineskin or Windbag? Elihu and the Problem of Justice in the Book of Job," *Ramify* 2, no. 1 (Spring 2001) 38–53.

Potgieter, Pieter C. "Perspectives on the Doctrine of Providence in Some of Calvin's Sermons on Job." *HTS Theological Studies* 54, nos. 1 & 2 (1998) 36–49.

Reitman, James. *Unlocking Wisdom: Forming Agents of God in the House of Mourning*. Springfield, MO: 21st Century, 2008.

Rogland, Max. "The Covenant in the Book of Job." *Criswell Theological Review* 7, no. 1 (Fall 2009) 49–62.

Rohr, Richard. *Job and the Mystery of Suffering: Spiritual Reflections*. New York: Crossroad, 1996.

Roper, Leon A., and Alphonso Groenewald, "Job and Ecclesiastes as (postmodern?) Wisdom in Revolt." *HTS Teologlese Studies/Theological Studies*, 69, no. 1 (2002) 1–8.

Schreiner, Susan E. *Where Shall Wisdom be Found? Calvin's Exegesis of Job from Medieval and Modern Perspectives*. Chicago: University of Chicago Press, 1994.

Schultz, Richard L. "Unity or Diversity in Wisdom Theology? A Canonical and Covenantal Perspective." *Tyndale Bulletin* 48, no. 2 (1987) 271–306.

Scott, Mark Stephen Murray. "Theodicy at the Margins: New Trajectories for the Problem of Evil." *Theology Today* 68, no. 2 (2011) 149–152,

Sider, Ronald J., John M. Perkins, Wayne L. Gordon, and F. Albert Tizon, *Linking Arms, Linking Lives: How Urban-Suburban Partnerships Can Transform Communities*. Grand Rapids: Baker, 2008.

Sine, Tom. *The New Conspirators: Creating the Future One Mustard Seed at a Time*. Downers Grove: IVP, 2008.

Smith, Gary V. "Is There a Place for Job's Wisdom in Old Testament Theology?" *Trinity Journal* 13 (1992) 3–20.

Sorge, Bob. *Pain, Perplexity, and Promotion: A Prophetic Interpretation of the Book of Job* Greenwood, MO: Oasis House, 1999

Sovik, Atle O. "Why Almost all Moral Critique of Theodicies is Misplaced," *Religious Studies* 44, no. 4 (December, 2008) 479–84.

Sunquist, Scott W. *Understanding Christian Mission: Participation in Suffering and Glory*. Grand Rapids: Baker Academic, 2013.

Bibliography

Sur, Priyali. "Silent Slaves: Stories of Human Trafficking in India." *Women Under Siege Blog*, December 30, 2013, http://www. womenundersiegeproject.org/ blog/entry/silent-slaves-stories-of-human-trafficking-in-india

Swinton, John. *Raging with Compassion: Pastoral Responses to the Problem of Evil*. Grand Rapids: Eerdmans, 2007.

Tada, Joni Eareckson. "Hope . . . The Best of Things," in *Suffering and the Sovereignty of God*. Edited by John Piper and Justine Taylor. Wheaton: Crossway, 2006.

Thomas, Derek. *Proclaiming the Incomprehensible God: Calvin's Teaching on Job*. Scotland: Christian Focus, 2004.

Van Engen, Charles. "'Mission' Defined and Described." Pages 7–29 in *Missionshift: Global Mission Issues in the Third Millenium*. Edited by David J. Hesselgrave and Ed Stetzer. Nashville: B & H, 2010.

Vanhoozer, Kevin J. *Remythologizing Theology: Divine Action, Passion, and Authorship*. New York: Cambridge University Press, 2010.

Van Leeuwen, Raymonnd C. "Wealth and Poverty: System and Contradiction in Proverbs," *Hebrew Studies* 33 (1992) 25–36.

Venugopal, Nikhita. "Actors Read Biblical Book of Job to Commemorate Sandy Devastation." *DNAinfo* (December 9, 2013). http://www.dnainfo.com/new-york/20131209/red-hook/actors-read-biblical-book-of-job-commemorate-sandy-devastation.

Waltke, Bruce K. *The Book of Proverbs, Chapters 1–15*. Grand Rapids: Eerdmans, 2004.

Walton, John H. *Job: the NIV Application Commentary*. Grand Rapids: Zondervan, 2012.

Waters, Larry J. "Elihu's Theology and His View of Suffering," *Bibliotheca Sacra* 156 (April-June, 1999) 143–59.

———. "Missio Dei in the Book of Job." *Bibliotheca Sacra* 166:681 (Jan 2009) 19–35.

———. "Reflections on Suffering from the Book of Job." *Bibliotheca Sacra* 154 (October-December 1997) 436–51.

Weaver, Natalie Kertes. *The Theology of Suffering and Death: An Introduction for Caregivers*. New York: Routledge, 2013.

Weikart, Richard. *From Darwin to Hitler: Evolutionary Ethics, Eugenics, and Racism in Germany*. New York: Palgrave Macmillian, 2006.

West, Sonja. "The Man Who Was Thursday, the Nightmare of Modernity, and the Days of Creation." *Discovery Institute* (April 10, 2002). http://www.discovery.org/a/1145

Wharton, James A. *Job*. Louisville: Westminster John Knox, 1999.

Wiesel, Elie. *Night*. New York: Hill and Wang, 1958; translation, 2006

Wilkinson, David. *Christian Eschatology and the Physical Universe*. New York: T & T Clark International, 2010.

Williams, Andrew. "Political Lament and Political Protest." *Cambridge Papers*, 23, no. 1 (March 2014) 1–4.

Wright, Christopher J. H. "'According to the Scriptures.' The Whole Gospel in Biblical Revelation." *Evangelical Review of Theology* 33, no. 1 (January 2009) 4–18.

———. *The Mission of God: Unlocking the Bible's Grand Narrative*. Downers Grove: IVP Academic, 2006.

Wright, N. T. *Evil and the Justice of God*. Downers Grove: IVP, 2006.

———. *Surprised by Hope: Rethinking Heaven, the Resurrection, and the Mission of the Church*. New York: Harper, 2008.

Yancey, Philip. *Disappointment With God: Three Questions No One Asks About*. Grand Rapids: Zondervan, 1988.

Bibliography

———. *Where is God When It Hurts?* Grand Rapids, MI: Zondervan, 1990.

Zaspel, Fred. "Interview with Zach Eswine." *Books at a Glance* (November 11, 2014). http:// www.booksataglance.com/author-interviews/interview-with-zack-eswine-author-of-recovering-eden-the-gospel-according-to-ecclesiastes

Zylla, Phil C. *Virtue as Consent to Being: A Pastoral-Theological Perspective on Jonathan Edwards's Construct of Virtue.* Eugene: Pickwick, 2011.

———. *The Roots of Sorrow: A Pastoral Theology of Suffering.* Waco: Baylor University Press, 2012.

www.ingramcontent.com/pod-product-compliance
Lightning Source LLC
Chambersburg PA
CBHW071509150426
43191CB00009B/1458